SUPER GRAINS

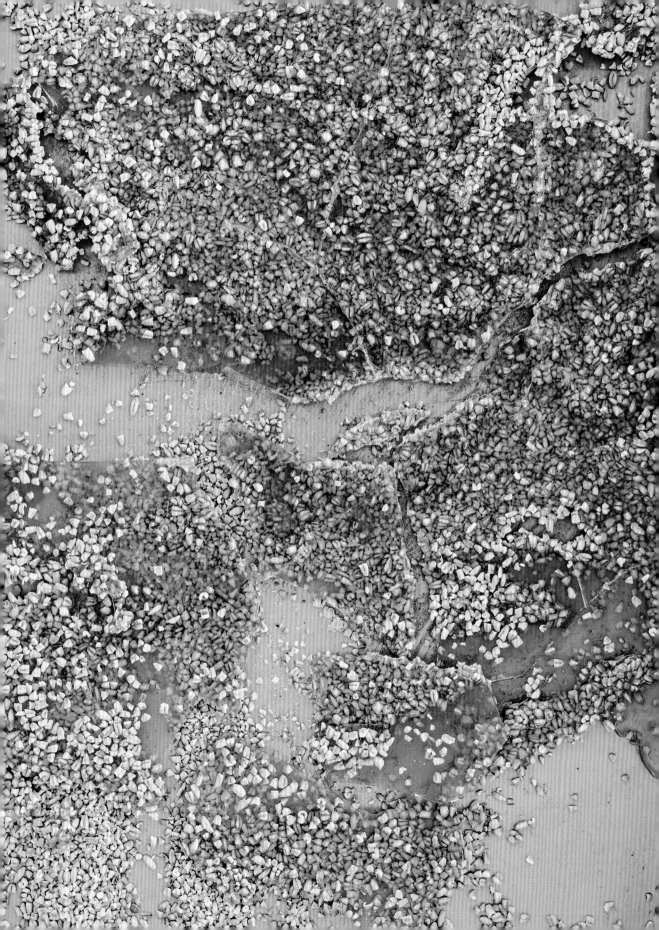

QUINOA•WHEAT•FARRO•SPELT
AMARANTH•BUCKWHEAT
BARLEY•CORN•WILD RICE
MILLET•TEFF•SORGHUM
CHIA•OATS•RICE•KAMUT
RYE•TRITICALE

JENNI MUIR

SUPER GRAINS

hamlyn

CONTENTS

Introduction   6

The recipes   12

Breakfast cereals   14
Pancakes & waffles   27
Breads   34
Soups   48
Salads   56
Couscous & pasta   68
Fritters & burgers   76
Polenta   81
Risottos   86
Stews   92
Grain-based stuffings for chicken   103
Other main courses   104
Mixed crumb coatings   110
Side dishes   111
Desserts   125
Cakes   138
Cookies & crackers   148
Snacks & sweets   157
Basic recipes   160
Supergrains directory   164
Further fields   180

Charts   184

Cooking guide   184
Nutritional facts   186
Sprouting   188

Index   189

Acknowledgements   192

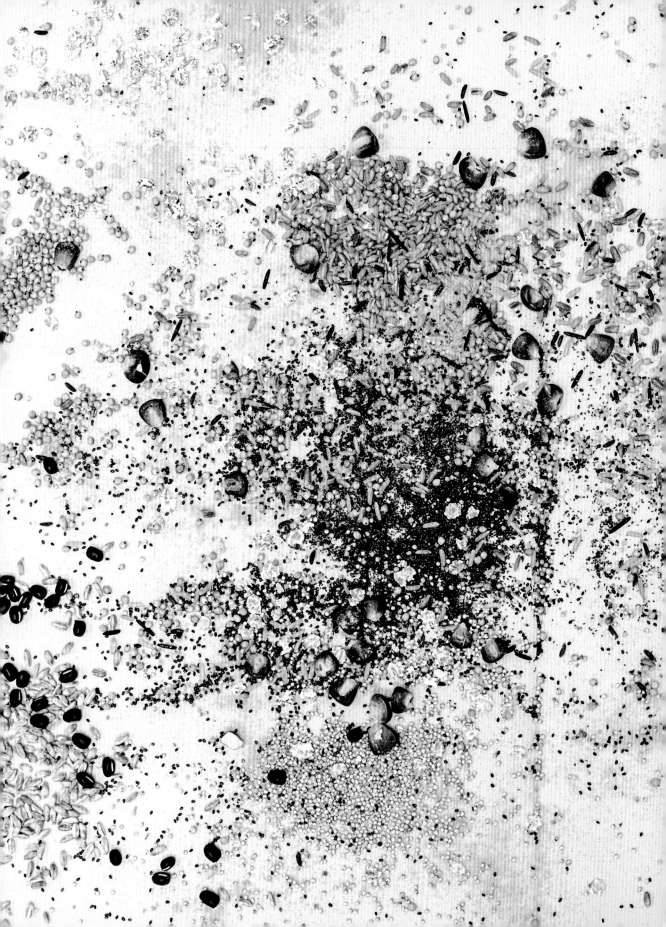

INTRODUCTION

Embracing wholegrains is one of the smartest things you can do for your health, your wallet and the planet. If you want to feel virtuous, look no further. These nutritional powerhouses are much more than mere staples and the variety of grain tastes and textures now available from around the world is fascinating, proving that eating well in the 21st century is not just about good health, it's about good taste, too.

INTRODUCTION

Grains are

nourishing, energising, inexpensive, comforting, robust, versatile, convenient

You probably need to include more wholegrains in your diet and I'm here to help you do that. Got a saucepan? Great, that's all you need to get started. What follows here is a personal tour of the wide world of cereal grains, plus seeds that we treat like grains in the kitchen and some other super things that are granular. I know you are going to be so enthused by the incredible variety of tastes, textures and amazing health benefits of these natural and traditional foods that you're going to want to race right down to the nearest trendy organic store and buy everything you can see, but I want you to **STOP RIGHT THERE.** Just pick two. Seriously. Try them a few different ways. If you like them, buy them again – and try another one as well. Get to know them gradually. Some will appeal more than others. Our aim here is to include a wider variety of wholegrains in your diet, not to have a wide variety of wholegrains sitting uneaten in the cupboard.

It doesn't matter which two you choose to start with, but I have a couple of suggestions:

1   Make sure that one of them is a proper whole- grain. Intact. Not pulverized, not ground, not puffed, not rolled, not pearled, not made into pasta or crackers or breakfast cereal. A bag of little pointed oval or round seeds. These have the important bran and germ layers hiding the starchy endosperm inside, slowing your digestion so that you feel full longer and avoid spikes in blood sugar.
2   The other should be quick to cook – a tender wholegrain such as quinoa or buckwheat, perhaps, or something that's been minimally processed to get it on the table faster, such as quick-cook farro or barley couscous. We all need

staples that help get us through the morning/ day/week – there's nothing wrong with that. We just want to mix them up a little and try and make them healthier.

The next step is to think about varying the foods you already know you like eating. When you go shopping, swap your usual loaf of bread for one made from spelt, rye or barley, for example. And the week after, choose another one again. If you normally use white pasta, pick up a bag of wholewheat, Kamut or corn spaghetti (truly the best option if you are looking for something gluten-free). Try brown rice or cornmeal porridge once a week instead of your staple oatmeal. Then use your oatmeal to make something savoury for dinner. It really is that easy.

Grains and health
Variety isn't just the spice of life; it's the stuff of life too. For maximum nourishment we need to embrace the huge diversity of ingredients nature has to offer. Japan led the way in this respect years ago, advising the public that they should aim to eat 30 or more different types of food from across six food groups each day, while also balancing calorie intake with energy expenditure.

One of the reasons an increasing number of people develop and suffer food intolerances (or food hypersensitivity) is the lack of variety in their diets. Too many people in the West eat a processed wheat breakfast cereal in the morning, a wheat bread sandwich for lunch and spaghetti (more wheat) for dinner. Such a diet can be moderate in terms of fat and calories, but it does not incorporate a variety of foods nor maximize nutrients. Exploring the range of grains available – whole, ground into flours or minimally processed into convenient foods such as pasta – will help you do that.

Grains are important sources of many nutrients, several of which are vital to good health. Key among these is fibre or 'roughage', which is only found in plant foods. Dietary advice on how much fibre we should consume differs between countries, and between life stages – pregnancy and lactation, for example, increase a woman's requirements. The United States National Academy of Sciences Institute of Medicine's recommendation is for 20–35g/¾–1½oz of fibre per day for adults; the UK's 18g/½oz per day for healthy adults seems a tad low.

Fibre passes undigested through the stomach and small intestine. On a basic level, it 'keeps you regular', but it also has many less obvious health benefits. Soluble fibre, which dissolves in water to form a thick gel, keeps the bowel healthy, helps prevent cancer, lowers blood cholesterol levels and therefore helps reduce the risk of heart disease. It is especially helpful for diabetics because it slows the release of sugars in the blood. Insoluble fibre helps push soluble fibre through to the colon, and prevents constipation and related problems such as haemorrhoids and diverticulitis. It also reduces the risk of colon cancer. Another type of fibre is resistant starch. Like insoluble fibre, it leaves the bowel undigested and is thought to reduce the risk of cancer, help control diabetes and encourage the growth of beneficial bacteria.

Wholegrain foods are higher in fibre than processed grains, which is why it is recommended that we eat some wholegrain foods daily. However, we also know now that wholegrains contain other beneficial nutrients such as phytoestrogens that protect against some forms of cancer and heart disease, and may relieve menopausal symptoms. The phytic acid found in the bran of the grain may protect against some cancers, while the phytosterols in cereal oils can reduce blood cholesterol.

To make dietary advice easier to understand, grains have traditionally been categorized as carbohydrate foods, in particular complex carbohydrates. However, this oversimplifies the issue. Even if we set aside the trendy high-protein, lysine-rich seed grains featured in this book and concentrate on the main cereal grasses – wheat, rye, barley, oats, rice, millet, sorghum and corn – it is apparent that grains are major sources of protein. If these eight cereal grains were your sole source of food (which they should not be), you would be consuming more protein than the body requires and your fat intake would be undesirably low.

On average, these species provide 45 per cent of the world's dietary protein and 50 per cent of its total food energy. The old argument that cereal grains are 'incomplete proteins' and have a 'lower biological value' compared to animal proteins is just that – old. The other foods we eat during the day – beans and pulses, nuts and seeds, meat and dairy products – complement the nutritional benefits of grains, making the total protein consumed 'complete'.

Even the Ancient Greeks knew that high-fibre wholegrain foods were beneficial for health and ate them as needed. Chinese and Indian traditions of food-health also consider grains to be essential health-promoting staples, but their specific recommendations are quite different from those given by Western medicine and nutrition practitioners. India's Ayurvedic system considers that whole, processed and refined grains all have a place in the diet and the choice at each meal should depend on the individual's body type, their current state of health and the season. As Ayurvedic culinary expert Miriam Kasin Hospodar suggests in her book *Heaven's Banquet*, a key reason many health food advocates have only promoted unrefined wholegrains in the past is in reaction to the widespread over consumption of highly refined grains and grain products. 'The important things to look for are, first, as always, that the grains are organically farmed and, second, how and why they have been processed,' she says. 'Some grains are refined to make them more digestible, making their nutrients more accessible. Grains with a heavy husk, such as barley and rice, are hard to digest and their pearled counterparts are the better Ayurvedic choice.'

The key message here is that there are many ways to health and most of us would be better off eating some unprocessed whole grain foods regularly. Maybe not always, but more often. Aim to add just a 50g/2oz (uncooked measure) of wholegrains to your daily food intake and you will slightly overshoot the recommended amount per day, while also reducing your risk of heart disease by up to 30 per cent, steadying your blood sugar and making meals more satisfying and sustaining.

Grains in the kitchen

Grains are wonderful natural foods, and mice and beetles love them. When you get your grains home, and certainly once you've opened the packet, put them in an airtight box or jar. I tend to use Lock & Lock 1.8-litre/3-pint upright classic containers because they are space efficient, stackable, easily take a new bag with the last of the old one, and I can use a 50g/2oz measure to scoop out the number of portions I need without hassle. Keep them in a dark, dry place and your wholegrains will last ages – that was much of their appeal for ancient peoples. Wholegrain and stoneground flours, on the other hand, stale quickly, so depending on when you think you'll use them, you may want to store them in the fridge or freezer.

If you want to cook with tiny grains such as amaranth, quinoa and teff, you will need a very fine mesh sieve to rinse and drain them before cooking. Occasionally I find that a bag of spelt, freekeh or posole needs picking through to remove stones, random seeds and other debris, in which case I tip a handful at a time onto a white plate to make the unwanted bits easier to see. It only takes a few minutes before cooking and is kind of relaxing. What's not relaxing is biting into gravel during dinner, but you do get to know brands and suppliers over time and can then make purchase decisions accordingly.

Despite what you may have read, presoaking grains is not generally necessary. Some believe it makes the grains' vitamin and mineral content easier to absorb by reducing phytic acid levels, but in household soaking conditions, the reduction of phytic acid levels is minimal. Others believe soaking kick-starts the germinating process, but unfortunately a lot of foods people think are whole- grains are not actually 'whole' and consequently are never going to germinate.

Soaking may shorten the cooking time of the grain, but you will soon decide for yourself which is more convenient: boiling for an extra 5–10 minutes, or remembering to soak the grain the day before cooking and then carrying through your plan to cook and eat it. I never presoak wholegrains, except the extraordinarily long-cooking varieties such as posole and rye berries.

I have included a chart (pages 184–185) for general guidance on cooking times, particularly when cooking grains plainly. These are, however, only approximations. Cooking times vary according to the degree of pearling or other processing, the age of the grain, its shape or variety, the method of cooking and what other ingredients are included in the pot.

Many suppliers overstate the length of cooking required on their packaging, and while it is worth noting their suggested times, it is also worth testing them 2–3 minutes sooner for quick-cooking grains and 10–15 minutes earlier for long-cooking grains. Rest assured that the more whole a grain is, the more difficult it is to overcook it. Long-cooking varieties are very forgiving and 5 or 10 minutes here or there makes little difference to the overall eating quality.

Cooked grains will keep for up to five days in a lidded container in the fridge. To reheat, put them in a covered saucepan with a 125ml/½ cup or so of water to generate steam and stir occasionally until they are soft and hot through. If you are using a microwave to reheat them, you don't need to add any water, just cover with a paper towel and cook on high, stirring occasionally.

I have never been so well organized but you can batch-cook packs of wholegrains and freeze them in convenient portions – thus allowing you to enjoy three months of ready-cooked nutrition from the freezer. If you have a microwave, you don't even have to remember to defrost the grains.

THE RECIPES

Cooking with grains is exciting. A simple bag of barley can take your tastebuds on a culinary journey from Morocco to Scotland via East Coast USA. What follows is an anthology of some of the world's best grain dishes with ideas and advice from great cooks all over. Whether you want indulgence or simplicity, fast food or leisurely cooking, purity or pure comfort, there is a recipe to suit any mood, any occasion and any lifestyle.

JOHN'S GRANOLA

My friend chef John Campbell won an award for offering the best hotel breakfast in the world, and this granola was part of his menu. Granola began life in the USA as 'granula', an invention of James Caleb Jackson, who baked a wholewheat flour and water mixture in sheets, then ground and rebaked them to serve with milk. Dr John Harvey Kellogg took inspiration from this and made a similar product he called granola from wheat, oats and corn.

SERVES 15

3 tbsp hazelnuts

325g/11oz rolled oats

125g/4oz barley flakes

100g/3½oz malted wheat flakes

30g/1¼oz wheatgerm

6 tbsp sultanas

3½ tbsp raisins

5 dried apricots, chopped

25g/1oz dried banana chips

3½ tbsp sunflower seeds

350–500g/11½oz–1lb runny
   Mexican honey

fresh fruit, to serve

Heat the oven to 180°C/350°F/Gas 4. Place the nuts on a large roasting tray and bake for 20 minutes or until golden, shaking them occasionally. Meanwhile, combine the grains, fruit and seeds in a large bowl.

Remove the nuts from the oven but do not turn it off. Leave the nuts to cool, then rub off the skins, chop the nuts roughly and add them to the dry ingredients, mixing well.

Spread the muesli out on the roasting tray and drizzle the honey evenly over it. Bake for 20–25 minutes, stirring every 5 minutes to incorporate the honey and break up any large clusters. Remove the tray from the oven and keep stirring the granola every 5–10 minutes until it is cold. Store in an airtight container for up to 2 weeks.

COOK'S NOTES

✻ You want small clusters of granola, not a sticky mass – if the mixture looks more like the latter, simply return it to the oven for further toasting and stirring until the honey is absorbed.

✻ John is adamant about the use of organic Mexican honey and finds that when using other varieties the recipe does not work as much to his liking. Viscosity is definitely an issue – the thicker the honey is, the more you will seem to require because it won't spread well. Try warming set or crystallized honey before use so that it coats the cereal lightly and evenly.

✻ Substitute all or part of the honey with maple syrup if desired. Some people prefer a half-and-half combination of honey and an oil such as sesame, corn or sunflower oil, which will lend a fattier flavour to the granola. You could also skip the honey and toasting process altogether, giving a homemade version of packaged muesli.

✻ When it comes to the dry ingredients, granola is highly flexible. A little more or less of this or that here and there really doesn't matter, and you should feel confident experimenting. For showing off, think dried cherries and almonds; in tropical mode, choose shredded coconut and dried mango. Chewy Medjool dates will lend a healthy toffee-flavoured richness, and sesame seeds a delicious nutty taste. If Zen purity is your aim, consider adding roasted and ground soya beans and a few tablespoons of linseeds. Add any fresh fruit, such as raspberries, when serving.

✻ Replacing the wheatgerm with psyllium husks (which are, let's face it, not hugely delicious or easy to eat) is a good way to vary the diet, while also making sure that you consume plenty of colon-friendly insoluble fibre.

CORNMEAL PORRIDGE

Wherever maize, or corn, has been adopted outside Mexico, turning it into porridge seems to have been a priority. South Africa has mealiepap, Italy polenta, Romania mamaliga, the USA mush or grits. At an international level, the popularity of cornmeal porridge is rivalled only by oatmeal but, unlike oatmeal, the basic combo of ground corn, water and salt, whether served hot or cold, sweet or savoury, is considered by several cultures to be appropriate for any time of day. For a hot breakfast it's ideal: quick, easy, versatile and inexpensive.

PER PERSON

50g/2oz cornmeal
a pinch of salt
450ml/¾ pint hot water, just boiled
milk, sugar and butter, to serve

Place the cornmeal and salt in a small, heavy saucepan. Pour the hot water over the cornmeal, stirring constantly with a long-handled wooden spoon or wire whisk to prevent lumps forming.

Bring the mixture to the boil, then reduce the heat right down and cook gently for 15–20 minutes, stirring very frequently but standing well back to avoid the hot, geyser-like spitting of the porridge. Add more hot water from the kettle when the mixture becomes thick and dry. The 'correct' consistency is the one you prefer, but aim first for a texture like the soft-peak stage of whipping cream, but denser.

Serve as is with milk, sugar and a tiny bit of butter, or flavour as desired. Allow the porridge to cool for a short time before eating; it has an extraordinary ability to retain heat.

COOK'S NOTES

- Butter is the magic ingredient that transforms cornmeal porridge into something delicious. You need only a tiny, tiny amount, but it makes a big, big difference.
- South African food expert Peter Veldsman advises that those unused to cornmeal porridge should first try it made with milk rather than water.
- Fruit is a good addition. You could simply serve with a ready-made compote, or mix in a handful of fresh or dried blueberries and the grated zest and juice of half a lemon. A tub of lemon yogurt folded through is nice, too, though you may still want to add some milk.
- For Jamaican-style porridge, use 225ml/7½fl oz water, 175ml/6fl oz cows' milk and 50ml/2fl oz coconut cream. Flavour with nutmeg, cinnamon and vanilla, and serve topped with coconut flakes and dark muscovado sugar. Chopped banana or dried mango also works well with this.
- My friend Claire Clifton, who grew up in Texas, would add a handful of diced tangy cheese such as feta or mild goats' cheese and fresh herbs. Other good savoury inclusions are chopped spring onions, ham or fried chorizo.
- Like to go to work on an egg? Poach one while the cornmeal is cooking and serve it on top, sprinkled with truffle oil and finely grated Parmesan.
- This is also the technique used to make porridge from Maltabella and other fine meals such as millet and barley. Dorothy Hartley reports in her book *Food in England* that barley meal makes the best milk porridge. In Tunisia, a sweet millet porridge known as sahlab is served at night, flavoured with orange blossom water, ginger and cinnamon or dried rose petals.

OATMEAL PORRIDGE

Good 'oatmeal' requires meal, not rolled flakes. Whenever someone says 'Wow! That's the best porridge I've ever eaten!', as though delicious porridge were an amazing rather than an everyday thing, it tends to be because the cook or chef has used proper oatmeal. According to Scots food expert Catherine Brown, this means medium oatmeal, sometimes with pinhead (or coarse, steel-cut oatmeal) added to give a rougher texture. 'Fine oatmeal produces too smooth a porridge for Scottish tastes,' she says. Instant oat flakes are just awful.

PER PERSON

50g/2oz medium oatmeal, or a mixture
    of medium and coarse oatmeal
about 300ml/½ pint water
a pinch of salt

Place the oatmeal in a small, heavy saucepan and toast it over a medium-low heat for 2–3 minutes, stirring constantly with a wooden spoon or Scottish spurtle, until lightly fragrant.

Slowly mix in the water (it may spit a little) and salt. Lower the heat right down and cook, stirring occasionally, for 20–30 minutes, depending on how crunchy or thick you like the oatmeal. If it becomes too thick, simply add a little more water.

COOK'S NOTES

✳ You'll notice that this mixture is not made with milk or a blend of half milk and half water. The dairy element comes at serving time.

✳ The 'right' or traditional way to serve porridge in Scotland is to place the cooked cereal in a wooden bowl to keep it hot, and sit a bowl of cold milk or cream alongside. A carved horn spoon is dipped into the porridge, then into the milk or cream, the idea being to enjoy the combination of hot and cold sensations until the last gloop of porridge is eaten.

✳ Tried and trusted sweeteners for porridge include golden syrup, molasses, maple syrup, honey and brown or white sugar. My friend Claire Clifton uses pomegranate molasses plus blueberries and crème fraîche – yum.

✳ A bowl of porridge topped with 1 tbsp whisky and 1 tbsp cream is a wonderful thing, especially on winter mornings, but I confess I prefer to use Cognac.

✳ The Scots tradition of leaving excess porridge to set, then cutting it into slices for eating cold or frying as an accompaniment to eggs, bacon or fish is not peculiar to Scotland. These and other ways of using leftover oatmeal can also be found in old American cookbooks. The best is perhaps oatmeal muffins (see Cook's Notes, page 34).

✳ At Sarabeth's restaurants, New York's definitive breakfast venues, oatmeal is a key feature of the menu. Cooked wheatberries are stirred into the porridge to give a crunchy mixture called Big Bad Wolf, which is served with cream, butter and brown sugar.

✳ If you like the big flavour of buckwheat, include a tablespoonful and don't skimp on the salt. Maple syrup is the sweetener of choice in this case. Teff grains are another good addition.

✳ Please be wary of relying on ready-made porridges from fast food chains, and pimped oat products from food processors. What is their fat and sugar content? Your daily fare needs to be wholesome, and a bit of oat dust in these mixtures doesn't make them so.

BROWN RICE AND MISO PORRIDGE WITH PEARS AND WALNUTS

This is my version of a staple of Peter Gordon's breakfast menu at The Providores and Tapa Room in London, where it is usually made with apples and served with a dollop of tamarillo compote. It is fabulously healthy yet indulgent too – go easy on the maple syrup if you're watching calories. Shiro miso is pale blond in colour and sweet in flavour. It's extremely versatile, making a lovely ice cream as well as the more usual savoury soups and dressings.

SERVES 2

100g/3½oz whole short-grain rice
2 tbsp walnut pieces
2 pears
150ml/¼ pint maple syrup
200ml/7fl oz soya milk or almond milk
1 heaped tbsp shiro miso (sweet white miso)

Wash the rice, then put it in a small saucepan and cover generously with water. Bring to the boil, reduce the heat to a simmer and cook the rice for 30 minutes or until fully tender. Top up the pan with extra hot water during cooking if the water level falls below the surface of the rice.

Meanwhile, toast the walnut pieces in a dry frying pan or the oven until they are fragrant. Transfer them to a dish to cool so that they don't scorch in the residual heat. Chop coarsely if you prefer smaller pieces of walnut.

Using a vegetable peeler, peel 4 or 5 strips of skin from each pear to give a striped effect. Halve or quarter the fruit and remove the cores. Put the flesh in a small saucepan with the maple syrup and bring to the boil. Reduce the heat to very low and cook for 5–10 minutes, stirring occasionally.

When the rice is ready, drain in a sieve and rinse under cold running water. Set the rice aside to drain thoroughly while you clean the saucepan.

Return the rice to the saucepan with the milk and heat until piping hot. Take a small ladle of hot milk and stir it into the shiro miso to make a thin paste, then pour the miso into the saucepan. Stir over the heat for a further 1–2 minutes.

Divide the milky rice among serving bowls. Spoon the pears and maple syrup over the rice and sprinkle with the toasted walnuts.

COOK'S NOTES

* The soya milk can easily be swapped; the miso acts as a sort of leveller. Peter suggests rice milk, and I've used both almond and cows' milks successfully.
* Mildly sweet grains such as barley, spelt, millet and quinoa work well, but brown rice is easily the best. Brown basmati, though not as plump as the short-grain, works a treat and cooks 5–10 minutes faster, which, even on Sunday mornings, can be persuasive.

STICKY BLACK RICE WITH COCONUT AND TOFU

Tell people you like tofu and they're likely to think you're weird. But they won't have had it freshly made, scooped warm and junket-like from the vat, the soya milk from which it's produced adding just a faint flavour and aroma. This is how I have enjoyed tofu in Japanese Kansai-style restaurants, where it was made in the centre of the table, and at Malaysian market stalls. The following recipe is from the latter, where it was sold with vividly coloured rice porridge and coconut cream as a sweet snack for any time of the day.

PER PERSON

50g/2oz black sticky (glutinous) rice
about 300ml/½ pint water
1 tbsp palm sugar
3–4 tbsp coconut cream, or more as desired
a pinch of salt
100g/3½oz silken tofu

Place the rice, water and palm sugar in a small, heavy saucepan and stir to dissolve the sugar. Bring to the boil over a medium-high heat, then reduce the heat right down and simmer for 25–35 minutes, stirring occasionally. Cook for longer if preferred, adding more water to achieve the desired consistency.

Meanwhile, in another small saucepan, beat together the coconut cream and salt until smooth. Place over a low heat and cook gently, stirring occasionally, until warmed through but not boiling.

Place the tofu on a small plate and lay inside a steamer. Set the steamer over a pan of water and bring to the boil, then lower the heat and steam the tofu for 3–5 minutes until hot.

To serve, place the hot tofu in a large serving bowl. Ladle the black rice porridge over the top of the tofu and drizzle with the warmed coconut cream.

COOK'S NOTES

✤ The closest approximation your grocer will have to the style of freshly made tofu required here is chilled fresh silken tofu. I can't stand the packaged taste of long-life tofu, no matter how many Southeast Asian people tell me it's good stuff. Never use firm pressed chewy tofu for this dish.

✤ This recipe is also suitable for black barley, which is available from some specialist grain suppliers and fondly remembered by Southeast Asian expatriates that I've met in London.

✤ The Malaysian woman at the market stall routinely soaked her black sticky rice overnight before cooking it until almost disintegrated. I tend to prefer the grains still reasonably whole, and have skipped the soaking with no horrifying extension of cooking time. Whatever degree of softness you choose, the mixture retains a slight crunch because of the bran on the rice.

✤ Sticky black rice and coconut can be combined differently to make a richer porridge suitable for indulgent mornings or a healthy dessert. You simply boil the rice in water until tender, then drain and place it in a saucepan with 225ml/7½fl oz coconut milk, 1 tbsp palm sugar, 2 tsp white sugar and a pinch of salt. Cook gently until thick, then serve drizzled with a little extra coconut milk or coconut cream.

FARRO WITH APRICOTS, POMEGRANATE AND PINE KERNELS

This dish is based on an Egyptian recipe in Rena Salaman's inspiring book *Healthy Mediterranean Cooking*. It is slightly reminiscent of a Jewish dish called belila, and a Jain one called chunna, a speciality of Rajasthan served garnished with gold or silver leaf. Even without the sparkly garnish, this is an indulgent combination, rich enough to be served as a dessert yet deceptively easy to make. The pomegranate adds a welcome note of juiciness.

SERVES 2–3

50g/2oz semi-pearled wheatberries such
    as farro
40g/1½oz pine kernels
175ml/6fl oz milk, plus extra to serve,
    if desired
2 tsp honey
1 tsp sugar
7 dried apricots, chopped
the seeds of ¼–½ pomegranate
2 tbsp flaked almonds
1 tsp rosewater, or to taste

Place the grains in a large pan of water and bring to the boil. Reduce the heat and simmer for 25–35 minutes or until tender. Drain thoroughly.

Meanwhile, if desired, toast the pine kernels in a dry frying pan for 3–5 minutes, stirring constantly, until golden and fragrant. Remove to a bowl to cool.

Clean out the pan that you used for cooking the wheat. Combine the wheat, milk, honey and sugar in the pan and bring to the boil. Reduce the heat and simmer for 10–15 minutes.

Remove the pan from the heat and stir in the pine kernels, apricots, pomegranate and almonds. Sweeten to taste with rosewater. Serve immediately, with additional milk if desired.

COOK'S NOTES

❖ Use wholegrain wheatberries of any type if preferred, boiling them in the pan of water for the necessary extra time to reach tenderness.

❖ Large-grained Kamut, derived from an ancient Egyptian wheat, would be an amusing choice, though you might want to chop the grains roughly before combining.

❖ This recipe is also your blueprint for other flavoured grain porridges: quinoa, teff, rice, barley, whatever. You want to add something nutty, toasty and crunchy; a fresh fruit element; a more intense and chewy dried fruit; plus a spicy note, which could be a different flower water or a pinch of ground spice. Swap the milk according to preference too.

❖ A reasonable version of the authentic Jain dish would be made from wheat, milk, sugar, a little ground cardamom and a few strands of saffron. Using Ebly, Pasta Wheat or pearled spelt rather than wholegrains would be most authentic here.

❖ Belila, according to Claudia Roden's *The Book of Jewish Food*, is made with young wholegrain wheat or pearl barley, and sugar syrup instead of milk. Flavourings would include orange flower water, cinnamon, pistachios, walnuts and soaked raisins or sultanas.

❖ These ingredients can be made into a terrific pudding. Cook the porridge as given here using 200g/1 cup wheat, 180g/6oz chopped dried apricots, 150g/5oz pine kernels, 35g/1½oz flaked almonds, 900ml/1½ pints milk, 2½ tbsp honey and 1 tbsp sugar. Whisk 2 eggs until light and fluffy, then slowly mix in a little hot milky porridge. Return to the saucepan and stir gently to combine. Spoon into a greased soufflé dish, sprinkle with a few flaked almonds and bake at 160°C/325°F/Gas 3 for about 30 minutes. Serve sprinkled with pomegranate seeds.

BIRCHER MUESLI

Raw oats for breakfast was not an idea entirely unique to Max Bircher-Benner, the Swiss physician credited with having invented this dish – the Scots beat him to it with their brose. The best-tasting bircher mueslis, especially those served in hotels, tend to include cream, which is not what most people who eat this regularly want in a breakfast. Interestingly, Dr Bircher-Benner's intention was not that his muesli be a high-grain dish but one that emphasized raw foods, especially fruit and nuts, which he believed made sick people better.

PER PERSON

2–3 tbsp rolled oats
1–2 tbsp sultanas or raisins
a little water or fruit juice, for soaking
1 apple
a squeeze of lemon juice
1 tbsp chopped unsalted nuts such
    as almonds, brazils or hazelnuts,
    or a mixture
1 tsp runny honey

To serve
2–3 tbsp natural plain yogurt
a handful of berries, halved if large

Place the oats and sultanas or raisins in a bowl and cover with a little water or fruit juice. Leave to soak overnight to plump and soften.

Just before serving, coarsely grate the apple, leaving the skin on. Stir the apple and the sweet juices it exudes into the oat mixture.

Mix in the lemon juice, nuts and honey, then serve the muesli with the yogurt, scattered with the berries.

COOK'S NOTES

❊ Grating an apple can seem heavy on effort early in the morning, but it is absolutely essential for flavour and juiciness. You could use a pear instead. A generous hand with the berries is another way to ensure a fine result.

❊ For the creamiest taste choose Greek yogurt or a mild bio yogurt, low-fat if you like. Use acidic-tasting yogurt with caution, unless, of course, you prefer it.

❊ Some people like to add ground cinnamon, ginger or nutmeg; I'm not one of them. I often forget to soak the oats overnight and make do by covering them with a little boiling water the next morning. By the time you've grated the apple and mixed in the other ingredients, the muesli is cool enough to eat and the oats are well softened.

❊ An idea from chef Adam Palmer when he was at Champney's health spa is to make a similar type of muesli with bulgur wheat. He boils 50g/2oz bulgur with 5 tbsp sugar, 1 tsp ground cinnamon, ½ tsp ginger, the zest and juice of an orange, plus 200ml/7fl oz soya milk, until the liquid has been absorbed and the grains are tender. Then he stirs in almonds, diced red and green apples and pears, and tops this mixture with a simple blackcurrant and honey compote. Very glamorous.

❊ To make Scots brose, place a portion of oat, barley or peasemeal in a heatproof bowl and cover with hot milk or water. Stir in some salt and a little butter, plus dried fruit if desired. It is also traditional to use leftover cooking water from meat or vegetables in this dish.

FINNISH OVEN PORRIDGE

The Scandinavian method of cooking porridge in the oven is one of the best ways of producing a cooked wholegrain cereal. I include it here because, while it might seem impractical for commuters to make, the many people who now work from home could find that it fits easily into their lifestyle. Put it in the oven on waking, shower, go out and buy the papers, and before you know it, there's a hot, healthy porridge ready to tuck into. In Finland this porridge is called uunipuuro and it is believed to make children grow strong.

SERVES 2–3

100g/3½oz semi-pearled or pot barley
175ml/6fl oz milk
175ml/6fl oz water
¼ tsp salt
a little butter and sugar, to serve

Heat the oven to 180°C/350°F/Gas 4. Combine the barley, milk, water and salt in an ovenproof dish. Bake for 1½–2 hours or until most of the liquid has been absorbed and the grains are full-blown and tender. Check the mixture about two-thirds of the way through cooking and add some extra milk or water if it is becoming too dry.

Remove from the oven and give the porridge a stir. Ladle into bowls and mix in butter and sugar to taste. Leftovers can easily be reheated for consumption the next day.

COOK'S NOTES

❉ You can easily substitute semi-pearled wheatberries, brown rice or coarse steel-cut oats for the barley in this recipe.
❉ In Poland a similar and surprisingly tasty dish is made using buckwheat kernels and cream. It includes a dash of vanilla essence, rum and a strip of lemon peel to flavour the mixture, and is best served sprinkled with icing sugar and fresh cherries. These additions really lighten the earthy, meaty taste of the buckwheat.

BRETON CREPES

Crêpes are often considered to be difficult to make, yet they are simple and demand merely that you observe a few rules. A non-stick pan really helps, so does a good bit of wrist action while pouring the batter, which must rest for 30 minutes before cooking. You might want to use clarified butter for greasing the pan – always, always lightly – as it will prevent scorching. The first one is unlikely to work out: just accept it and let it be.

SERVES 4

50g/2oz plain wheat-type flour
50g/2oz buckwheat flour
a pinch of salt
2 eggs
225ml/7½fl oz milk
25g/1oz butter
a little butter or vegetable oil spray,
    for greasing

Sift the wheat flour, buckwheat flour and salt into a large mixing bowl. Make a well in the centre and break in the eggs. Whisk until the eggs are broken up thoroughly. Gradually add the milk, whisking to a smooth batter, then set aside for 30 minutes.

Meanwhile, melt the butter and stir it into the batter just before cooking.

Place a steel or non-stick crêpe pan (about 18cm/7in in diameter) over a medium-high heat until it is very hot. The pan is ready for cooking when a drop of water bounces on the surface. If the water just lies there, the pan is not hot enough; if it quickly evaporates, it is too hot.

When ready, lightly grease the pan. Lift the pan off the heat with one hand and use the other to pour a small ladle of batter into the pan, while turning and tilting the wrist of the other hand to ensure the batter spreads lightly and evenly over the base of the pan.

Cook the crêpe for 1–2 minutes or until the top side is set and the underside is browned. Using a palette knife, lift up the side of the crêpe and ease the palette knife under. Flip over the crêpe and continue cooking on the other side until done. Set aside on a plate while you cook the rest of the batter, stacking the crêpes as you go.

COOK'S NOTES

❉ Lemon juice and sugar are for me the best accompaniments by far. For a hearty savoury dish, break an egg onto the uncooked side while the crêpe is cooking, and let it 'fry'. When just set, sprinkle with a little finely grated Gruyère cheese and some pepper, and roll up.
❉ Decreasing the milk in this recipe by ½fl oz will give a thicker pouring batter suitable for batter puddings such as clafoutis, Yorkshire pudding and toad-in-the-hole.
❉ Buckwheat-based batter is especially good for clafoutis, which is traditionally made by laying a cup or so of Griottines (marinated sour cherries) in the base of an ovenproof dish and covering them with the batter. A terrific alternative is 5 quartered plums marinated in 4 tbsp maple syrup. Bake at 180°C/350°F/Gas 4 for about an hour.
❉ For very delicate lacy crêpes, use cornflour (cornstarch) in place of the buckwheat flour.

QUINOA AND CHIA PANCAKES WITH MANGO AND BASIL COMPOTE

These pancakes are satisfying, so you'll probably be happy with just a couple. Frying them in coconut oil gives a lovely sweet aroma but, if you prefer, use 1-calorie Frylight (I'm a fan). Coconut milk yogurt is a superior (although expensive) dairy-free alternative.

SERVES 4

For the pancakes
100g/3½oz quinoa
300ml/½ pint water
200g/7oz white spelt flour
1 tbsp baking powder
½ tbsp sugar
2 tbsp chia seeds
175ml/6fl oz buttermilk
3 large eggs
½ tbsp vanilla extract
coconut oil or butter, for frying

For the compote
150ml/¼ pint agave syrup
½ vanilla pod, split
2 large juicy mangoes, peeled and sliced
2 tsp coconut oil or butter
6 basil leaves

To serve
coconut milk yogurt or other thick
    creamy yogurt
tiny basil leaves

Place the quinoa in a very fine sieve and rinse it thoroughly under cold running water. Put it in a saucepan and cover with the measured water. Bring to the boil, then reduce the heat and cover the pan. Simmer gently for 8 minutes, then turn off the heat under the pan and leave the quinoa to steam for a further 10 minutes. Tip it into a large mixing bowl and leave to cool.

Add the spelt flour, baking powder, sugar and chia seeds to the cooked quinoa and stir to combine. Whisk the buttermilk, eggs and vanilla together, then add them to the dry ingredients and stir to make a thick batter. Leave to stand for 20–30 minutes.

To make the compote, put the agave syrup in a saucepan. Scrape the seeds from the vanilla pod into the agave and throw in the husk. Gently warm through and add the mango flesh, including the scrappy bits. Heat through, stirring occasionally.

Preheat a large frying pan or griddle and heat the oven to 120°C/250°F/Gas ½ to keep the pancakes warm while you cook the remainder. Once the frying pan is hot, grease it lightly with coconut oil or butter and cook ladles of the batter, about 60ml/¼ cup per pancake, until brown on each side. Place on a baking tray and put in the oven.

When the batter is almost finished, stir the coconut oil or butter into the mango compote to enrich the fruity syrup. Tear up the basil leaves and stir them into the compote.

Stack the pancakes on serving plates, spooning a little syrup and some of the small fruit pieces between each layer. Top with the best-looking slices of mango and a scoop (or quenelle if you wish) of your preferred yogurt. Finish with the last of the syrup and tiny basil leaves.

COOK'S NOTES

❉ The mango compote is a health-conscious take on a Ken Hom classic. He cooks the fruit in sugar syrup, adds more butter and serves it with vanilla ice cream for dessert. Obviously you could replace it with any compote or fruit salsa that takes your fancy.

❉ Replace the quinoa with rice or millet, or with rolled oats that you've covered with boiled water.

GRIDDLE CAKES

Terrific pancakes drenched in maple syrup, and preferably served with bacon, are for many of us the culinary highlight of trips to the USA. We have the Dutch to thank for taking pancakes, as well as waffles and doughnuts, to the New World, but we also have them to blame for coleslaw. Much as I love pancakes, these days I find them flabby and bland when made from only white wheat flour; a proportion of buckwheat or cornmeal is almost compulsory for me, unless the recipe is particularly rich in eggs or features ricotta or curd cheese.

SERVES 3–4

75g/3oz buckwheat flour
50g/2oz plain wheat-type flour
2 tsp baking powder
1 tsp sugar
¼ tsp salt
3 eggs, separated
150ml/¼ pint milk
15g/½oz butter
a little butter or vegetable oil spray,
    for greasing

In a large bowl, combine the buckwheat flour, wheat flour, baking powder, sugar and salt. Stir to combine, then make a well in the centre.

Drop in the egg yolks and begin to slowly mix in the flour mixture. Gradually add the milk, stirring to a smooth batter, then set aside for 20–30 minutes.

Meanwhile, melt the butter ready to add to the batter. When almost ready to cook, whisk the egg whites in a large bowl until stiff peaks form.

Fold a large spoonful of the egg whites into the batter to lighten the mixture, then fold in the remaining egg white and melted butter.

Heat a griddle or large, heavy frying pan over a medium-high heat. Use a small ladle to add equal quantities of batter to the pan to make round pancakes. When bubbles have appeared on the surface and then popped, and the underside is a rich golden brown, flip the pancakes over and cook on the other side for 2–3 minutes. Serve immediately, or keep warm on a baking tray in a low oven while you finish cooking the rest of the batter.

COOK'S NOTES

✳ This isn't so much a recipe as a formula. You can use pretty well any grain flour or mixture of flours that you like in it, provided you stick with these basic proportions of wheat flour and complementary grain. You can also add 15g/½oz of a cooked grain such as millet or wild rice to the batter with no ill effects. To make blueberry or raspberry pancakes, simply press the fruit into the soft top side of the pancakes just after they go on the griddle.

✳ I have found this recipe, when made with buckwheat vastly superior to any authentic yeasted blini recipe I've tried, and much easier to cook. Don't hesitate to use this one when serving canapés of tiny pancakes topped with soured cream and smoked salmon or fish roe.

✳ For days when you don't fancy separating eggs and whisking the whites, simply stir 1 whole egg into this batter; it will then feed only 2, but it makes pancake day a real no-brainer.

WILD RICE WAFFLES

These are the best waffles I've ever eaten, bar none. The idea came from one of my favourite cookbooks, *Good Mornings*, by American food writer Michael McLaughlin. In it, he meticulously plans what steps to take the night before to ensure all his wonderful dishes are quickly and easily prepared in the morning, suggesting that he must be a lovely man to wake up with. Indeed, I can confirm the pulling power of these waffles and became so enthused of my dinky waffle machine that I upgraded to an expensive space-eating contraption insanely large for our kitchen.

MAKES 4

75g/3oz wild rice
20g/¾oz butter
100g/3½oz plain wheat-type flour
50g/2oz coarse yellow cornmeal
1 tbsp sugar
1 tsp baking powder
a large pinch of salt
1 egg
175ml/6fl oz milk
a little vegetable oil spray, for greasing
butter and maple syrup, to serve

Place the wild rice in a small saucepan, cover with a generous quantity of water and bring to the boil. Reduce the heat and simmer for 45 minutes or until the grains are butterflied and tender. Drain and rinse under cold running water. Set aside to drain thoroughly.

Melt the butter and set aside. Sift the wheat flour, cornmeal, sugar, baking powder and salt into a large mixing bowl. Make a well in the centre and crack in the egg, whisking to break it up. Gradually whisk in the milk and melted butter to give a smooth batter. Stir in the cooked rice.

Heat a waffle iron, preferably non-stick and electric, according to the manufacturer's instructions. Coat lightly with vegetable oil spray. Pour a large ladle of batter into the machine, or enough so that it is about three-quarters full, and clamp shut.

Cook for 3–4 minutes or until the waffle has browned and crisped to your liking. Keep warm in a low oven while you finish cooking the rest of the batter. Serve hot, topped with butter and maple syrup.

COOK'S NOTES

- Michael McLaughlin's recipe uses buckwheat flour instead of cornmeal, buttermilk in place of milk and oil in place of melted butter. Buttermilk is not easy to get in my area, so I use regular milk. You could sour it with 1 tsp lemon juice if desired.
- These waffles are good with black barley, millet or uncooked amaranth mixed in instead of the wild rice, but for me the wild rice version is definitely superior.
- Most pouring batter recipes, sweet or savoury, are suitable for cooking as waffles. The key difference between waffles and thick pancakes is that waffles require a little more fat to make them crisp.
- I've tried yeasted waffle batters and can't see the point of them. The batter doesn't need to puff up only to be squashed down again by the iron. All it does is make the waffles taste yeasty.

OLD-FASHIONED MUFFINS

These are what American muffins used to be before they became overblown fairy cakes loaded with chocolate bits, cherry streusel topping and poppy seeds. The original not-too-sweet, part-bread, part-scone style of mixture earned muffins a reputation as a healthy breakfast food, one that they still have, though tend not to deserve. They're the type of quick breads you whip up in the morning before getting stuck into a hard day of physical work, herding buffalo and so on, not frippery to nibble while chatting with the girls over cappuccino.

MAKES 15–20

190g/6½oz rye flour
190g/6½oz plain wheat-type flour
4 tsp baking powder
1 tsp salt
1 egg
4 tbsp molasses
275ml/9fl oz milk
15g/½oz butter, melted, plus extra for greasing

Heat the oven to 200°C/400°F/Gas 6 and grease some muffin trays or pans with butter. Sift the rye flour, wheat flour, baking powder and salt into a large mixing bowl and make a well in the centre.

In a jug, beat the egg and mix in the molasses and milk. Pour the milk mixture into the dry ingredients and stir briefly to give a smooth, thick batter. Quickly stir in the melted butter.

Divide the mixture among the greased muffin trays, baking in batches if necessary. Bake in the hot oven for 25 minutes. Serve hot, warm or cold.

COOK'S NOTES

✽ Let's be quite clear about this: these muffins taste richer than white-flour bakery items, but are nevertheless 'plain'. You are supposed to eat them with something else, such as butter, jam, apple sauce or the tasty juices left on the plate after a large breakfast of egg, sausages and bacon.

✽ Good cornmeal muffins are made following this method, but using 75g/3oz cornmeal, 150g/5oz plain wheat flour, 1 tbsp sugar, 1 tbsp baking powder, ½ tsp salt, 1 egg, 175ml/6fl oz milk and 1 tbsp melted butter.

✽ Strongly recommended as a use for leftover porridge are these oatmeal muffins. Sift 225g/7½oz flour, 2 tbsp sugar, 1 tbsp baking powder and ½ tsp salt into a bowl, then rub in 290g/9½oz cooked oatmeal until the mixture resembles coarse breadcrumbs. Beat together 120ml/4fl oz milk and an egg and stir them into the dry mixture, followed by 1 tbsp melted butter.

DUTCH HONEY CAKE

'Cake' here will be a misnomer to anyone familiar with the process of creaming butter and sugar until light and fluffy, then beating in an egg, plain flour and milk. This extraordinarily quick mixture has no butter, no eggs and uses rye flour. The effect is reminiscent of malt loaf rather than Madeira cake, so the recipe features in this section accordingly. In the Netherlands, it is traditionally eaten for breakfast with cheese and bread, something that will appeal to anyone who enjoys the combination of fruit cake and Wensleydale.

SERVES 10

butter, for greasing
300g/10oz rye flour
200g/7oz dark brown sugar
1 tsp baking powder
1 tsp ground cinnamon
½ tsp grated or ground nutmeg
½ tsp ground cloves
225ml/7½fl oz milk

Heat the oven to 180°C/350°F/Gas 4 and grease a loaf tin. Sift the rye flour, brown sugar, baking powder, cinnamon, nutmeg and cloves into a large mixing bowl and make a well in the centre.

Gradually stir the milk into the dry ingredients to give a smooth, thick batter. Pour the batter into the prepared loaf tin and bake for 1–1¼ hours until a skewer inserted in the centre comes out clean.

Remove from the oven and leave to stand in the tin for 15 minutes before turning out onto a wire rack to cool further. Wrap the cooled loaf in foil to store.

COOK'S NOTES

✳ Unlike other quick breads, but in common with many rye products, this loaf tastes better a few days after baking. Indeed, the extent to which it improves is quite astonishing.
✳ For a ginger version of this loaf, add a little ground ginger, plus 4–6 tbsp chopped glacé, crystallized or drained preserved stem ginger just before it goes into the loaf tin.
✳ For a fruity version, stir in 4 tbsp sultanas and 4 tbsp finely chopped pitted dates.
✳ This loaf is terrific spread with butter, and a great recipe to know when catering for people with wheat intolerance. You could also, if necessary, make it with water in place of milk.

CORN TORTILLAS

I know, I know, I know. To anyone who has enjoyed freshly baked tortillas in Mexico – big, puffy and (in my case) purple things that smell clearly and wonderfully of fresh corn – this recipe might seem a compromise too far. But even the increasing number of Mexican residents, restaurants and street food stalls in the UK has not yet resulted in the availability of truly fabulous tortillas. Masa harina is, however, a delightful ingredient to work with and readily available from Cool Chile and some branches of Sainsbury (look in the gourmet ingredients section).

MAKES 12

250g/8oz masa harina, plus extra
    for dusting
about 225ml/7½fl oz hot water

Take a thick plastic food storage bag and cut around the seams with scissors to give 2 tough sheets of plastic. Set aside until ready to press the tortillas.

Place the masa harina in a large bowl and make a well in the centre. Pour in most of the hot water and stir to incorporate the flour and give a soft but not sticky dough. Add more water if necessary.

Dust a work surface with extra masa harina. Turn the dough out onto it and knead lightly 5 or 6 times. Divide the dough into 12 equal pieces and shape each one into a ball. Cover them with a damp tea towel.

Take a ball of dough and place it between the sheets of plastic. Lay them in a tortilla press and close it. Move the handle from side to side to help flatten the ball until it is about 13cm/5in across. Open the press and turn the dough halfway round, then close and flatten again. Remove the tortilla from the plastic, retaining the plastic for the next one.

Place a griddle or large, heavy frying pan over a medium heat. When it is solidly hot, lay the tortilla on it and cook for 30 seconds. Flip it over and continue cooking on the other side for another 30 seconds or until little brown spots start to appear underneath. Flip it over again and continue cooking for a further 30–45 seconds, at which point the tortilla should puff up a little. Remove from the heat and keep warm while you press and cook the remaining tortillas.

COOK'S NOTES

✤ A tortilla press (a Spanish invention) is helpful, but not essential. Mexican cookery experts simply work the dough ball between their palms to flatten it. The rest of us can get by with a heavy frying pan and firm intentions.

✤ Authentic corn tortillas are smaller than the wheat flour tortillas sold for Tex-Mex cooking. You will need to serve 2 per person.

✤ For a terrific quick meal, fill the tortillas with a mixture of 300g/10oz boiled potatoes, cubed and sautéed in a little oil with 150g/5oz chopped chorizo, some dried oregano and salt.

✤ Another first-class treatment is to fill them with fresh white crabmeat and tomato salsa. Make a sauce by puréeing 150g/5oz pumpkin seeds with 225ml/7½fl oz fish stock until very smooth and thick. Heat the sauce gently in a pan, then spoon it over the warm filled tortillas.

NEW ORLEANS PAIN DE RIZ

'It has been said, and justly, that the only people who know how to make cornbread are the Southern people,' says *The Picayune's Creole Cook Book*, a collection of Louisiana-French recipes now over 100 years old. With characteristic pride it states: 'The Creoles, like all true Southerners, never use the yellow cornmeal for making bread, but always the whitest and best meal. In the South the yellow meal is only used to feed chickens and cattle.' This old-time bread is intended for breakfast, but in contemporary terms it would be better at brunch.

SERVES 9

150g/5oz white cornmeal
1½ tsp baking powder
½ tsp salt
90g/3½oz cooked white rice
2 eggs
340ml/12fl oz milk
5g/¼oz butter, melted, plus extra
    for greasing and serving

Heat the oven to 200°C/400°F/Gas 6 and grease a 20cm/8in square cake tin. Sift the cornmeal, baking powder and salt into a large mixing bowl. Rub the cooked rice into the meal until it resembles fine breadcrumbs. Make a well in the centre of the bowl.

Beat the eggs together in a jug and mix in the milk and melted butter. Stir the liquid ingredients into the mixing bowl, beating well to give a light batter.

Pour the mixture into the prepared tin and bake for 30 minutes. Remove from the oven and serve hot with lots of butter and preserves or alongside savoury foods with plenty of sauces and relishes.

COOK'S NOTES

✻ Despite the richness of this mixture, which features eggs, milk and butter, it is like many cornbreads in that it can be disconcertingly dry to those unused to the texture. That is why it is especially important to serve it with suitably saucy accompaniments and lots of butter.
✻ I've presented this cornbread to guests with sausages, bacon, eggs and mushrooms, plus plenty of homemade tomato sauce (see recipe for tomato sauce, page 162). Baked beans would be good too, as well as slices of roasted red bell pepper.
✻ Though I have not yet tried it, roast chicken and a creamy gravy also seem to me to be ideal partners for this bread.
✻ You could divide the batter between muffin trays or pans and bake them for 20–25 minutes to give individual cornbreads.

ORKNEY-STYLE BANNOCKS

To many people living outside Canada, it is surprising to learn that the historic Scots bannock is seen as good traditional fare of the First Nations peoples. They have been eating the simple unleavened griddle-baked bread, made with cornmeal rather than barley and wheat flours, since the 17th century when Scottish fur traders took the method to North America. Like Australia's damper and Africa's roosterkoek, the bannock requires few ingredients and can be easily cooked outdoors on a hot plate as well as baked in an oven.

MAKES 4

300g/10oz beremeal or barley flour, plus
    extra for dusting
150g/5oz plain wheat-type flour
1 tsp bicarbonate of soda
1 tsp cream of tartar
a pinch of salt
about 225ml/7½fl oz buttermilk

Place a griddle or heavy-based frying pan over a medium to low heat and leave to get hot.

Sift the beremeal, plain flour, bicarbonate of soda and cream of tartar into a large bowl to aerate the mixture, then stir in any remnants of bran from the beremeal. Make a well in the centre of the dry ingredients and work in just enough buttermilk to give a stiff dough.

Dust a work surface generously with flour and tip the dough out onto it. Divide the mixture into 4 even pieces and roll out each one in turn to give rounds about 3.5cm/1½in thick. Place on the hot griddle or in the pan and cook for 2–3 minutes on each side until the crust is browned and the inside is cooked. Serve immediately.

COOK'S NOTES

✣ If baking, heat the oven to 190°C/375°F/Gas 5 and bake for 20 minutes.
✣ You can use fine oatmeal or oat flour in place of the beremeal, or make the mixture entirely from fine white cornmeal.
✣ Some people like to work in 25g/1oz fat such as butter or lard, or a combination of the two. Rub them into the dry ingredients if using. The mixture can also be sweetened with a little treacle if liked.
✣ Serve with lots of butter and Cheddar cheese and a glass of beer.

BARLEY BREAD

The oldest pieces of bread found in Britain were from an archaeological pit in Oxfordshire and made of barley. When they were examined through the microscope, the partially crushed grains of barley were clearly visible and the bread was dated at around 5,500 years old. Although that loaf would have been coarse and leaden, this one based on a recipe by Martha Rose Shulman has a lovely light texture and slightly sweet taste.

MAKES 1 LARGE LOAF

225g/7½oz wholemeal wheat-type bread flour

185g/6½oz plain wheat-type bread flour, plus extra for dusting

100g/3½oz barley flour

½ tbsp salt

1 tsp active dried yeast

350ml/12fl oz lukewarm water

2 tbsp buttermilk

1 tbsp runny honey

1 tbsp vegetable oil, plus extra for greasing

1 small egg

2 tbsp water

1 tbsp sesame seeds

Place all the flours, plus the salt and yeast in a large mixing bowl. Stir to combine, then make a well in the centre. In a jug, whisk together the water, buttermilk, honey and oil, and pour the mixture into the dry ingredients. Gradually incorporate the flours into the liquid, working them together to give a soft, sticky dough.

On a well-floured work surface, knead the dough for 15 minutes until it firms up and becomes quite elastic. Shape it into a ball.

Wash the mixing bowl and dry it. Lightly grease the inside of the bowl with oil and place the ball of dough inside, turning it over to ensure it is coated in oil. Cover the bowl with clingfilm and then with a tea towel. Place in a warm spot and leave the dough to prove for 1½–2 hours or until it has doubled in size.

Punch the dough down and turn out onto a floured work surface. Knead briefly, shape into a cylinder and set aside for 10 minutes. Meanwhile, oil a loaf tin. Lay the smoothest side of the dough down into the tin, then turn it back up so that the seam in the dough is on the bottom. Whisk the egg with the water. Brush this over the top of the dough, sprinkle with the sesame seeds, then brush again with the egg glaze. Cover with a damp tea towel and set aside to prove again until the sides of the dough reach the rim of the tin and the top rises above it.

Heat the oven to 180°C/350°F/Gas 4. Use a small, sharp knife to slash diagonally across the top of the bread and bake for 50 minutes or until the loaf sounds hollow when tapped on the bottom. Cool on a wire rack.

COOK'S NOTES

✣ My version is lighter than Martha Rose Shulman's, the result of a happy accident in which I added too much plain wheat flour to the mixing bowl. It makes the bread less dense, which I don't intend as a criticism because I love heavy loaves and use her *Great Breads* book frequently. If you want a denser style, use 100g/3½oz plain wheat flour.

AMERICAS BREAD

This attractive Granary-style loaf combines the best of the American grains with the addition of potato. Although rich in wholesome ingredients, the finished bread is elegant and light, good for serving at stylish informal lunch parties, or when making sandwiches or toast. Despite what may seem like many steps and components, it's actually gratifyingly easy. The recipe is based on one from esteemed baker and caterer Beth Hensperger.

MAKES 1 LARGE LOAF

- 2 tbsp wild rice
- 175g/6oz potato, peeled and cubed
- 4 tbsp quinoa
- 15g/½oz butter
- 2 tbsp cornmeal
- 125ml/4fl oz milk
- 375g/12oz plain wheat-type flour, plus extra for dusting
- 75g/3oz wholemeal wheat-type flour
- 2 tsp active dried yeast
- 1 tbsp caster or granulated sugar
- 1½ tsp salt
- 2 tbsp pumpkin seeds
- 2 tbsp popped amaranth (see Cook's Notes)
- 4 tbsp rolled oats
- vegetable oil, for greasing

In a small pan of boiling water, cook the wild rice for 45 minutes or until tender. Meanwhile, in separate pans of water, boil the potato for 20 minutes or until tender, and simmer the quinoa for 12–15 minutes.

When cooked, drain the grains and spread them out on a plate to dry. Drain the potato, reserving 175ml/6fl oz of the cooking water. Mash the potato with the butter. Place the cornmeal in a small bowl and stir in the reserved cooking water.

Heat the milk gently until lukewarm. In a large mixing bowl, combine 150g/5oz of the plain flour with the wholemeal flour, yeast, sugar, salt and pumpkin seeds. Work in the mashed potato and wet cornmeal, then add the warm milk, popped amaranth, cooked wild rice and quinoa and mix well.

Gradually add the remaining 225g/7½oz, or more, of plain flour as required to give a soft but not sticky dough. Dust a work surface with flour and knead the dough for 5 minutes until elastic.

Wash and dry the mixing bowl and grease it with oil. Place the dough in it, then turn it over so that it is covered in oil. Cover with clingfilm and leave to rise for about 1½ hours or until the dough has doubled in volume.

Oil a loaf tin and dust the inside with the rolled oats. Punch down the risen dough, knead well, then shape into a loaf and lay it in the tin. Leave to rise for 40 minutes until just above the rim of the tin.

Heat the oven to 200°C/400°F/Gas 6. Bake the bread for 10 minutes, then reduce the heat to 180°C/350°F/Gas 4 and continue cooking for a further 30–35 minutes until the loaf is browned and sounds hollow when tapped on the base. Cool on a wire rack.

COOK'S NOTES

- To pop the amaranth yourself, add 1 tbsp of seeds to a hot frying pan and stir constantly with a natural-bristled brush until they pop, being careful not to let them burn (see Cook's Notes, page 151).

SOWETO GREY BREAD

Grey rather than brown, this partially wholemeal loaf from South Africa is a good stepping stone to full-on wholemeal bread for those reluctant to make the move. It's also a good first-time yeast bread for anyone new to baking. The quantity of yeast is comparatively high, so the bread rises well and quickly, making the proving process seem less intimidating to fledgling breadmakers. This short-sharp-shock method is treated with disapproval by some bakers, but is beneficial in the hot climate from which the recipe originates.

MAKES 1 LARGE LOAF

250g/8oz plain wheat-type flour,
    plus extra for dusting
100g/3½oz whole wheat-type flour
10g/½oz active dried yeast
1 tsp caster or granulated sugar
1 tsp coarse sea salt, plus extra to glaze
225ml/7½fl oz lukewarm water
20g/¾oz butter, plus extra for greasing
    mixing bowl
2–3 tbsp poppy seeds
1 tsp cornflour

In a large bowl, combine the 2 flours, yeast, sugar and salt. Mix in the water and work into a dough, adding more water as necessary to give a soft but not sticky dough.

Grease your palms well with some of the measured butter and knead the dough in the bowl for 5 minutes. Butter your hands again and knead the dough some more. Continue buttering your hands and kneading until the measured butter is used up and you have been kneading for about 15 minutes.

Grease the mixing bowl with additional butter. Shape the dough into a ball, place it in the bowl, then turn so that the top is greased. Cover with clingfilm and leave to prove in a warm place for 10 minutes; the dough should be allowed to rise, but not so much that it doubles in volume.

Punch down the dough, then knead it again briefly. Turn the dough out onto a floured work surface and roll it into a square. Sprinkle the poppy seeds over the top of the dough and press them in very gently. Carefully roll up the dough like a Swiss roll to enclose the poppy seeds. Cover with clingfilm and leave in a warm spot until doubled in size, about 20 minutes.

Heat the oven to 200°C/400°F/Gas 6 and place the loaf on a floured baking sheet. In a mixing bowl, combine the cornflour with 1 tsp salt and 2 tsp water, stirring to make a paste. Brush over the top of the loaf and bake for 5 minutes, then lower the heat to 180°C/350°F/Gas 4 and continue cooking for a further 40 minutes until the loaf is browned and well risen.

COOK'S NOTES

❋ The poppy seeds can be omitted, in which case the dough simply needs to be kneaded again and then shaped as desired. You could also use chia or sesame seeds in place of poppy.

❋ Alternatively, mix the poppy seeds into a chopped onion fried in butter until soft and golden. Cool and spread this mixture over the uncooked dough before rolling it up.

NORWEGIAN FLATBRØD

Flatbrød is the national bread of Norway. It is a thin, crisp cracker bread made from flours such as rye and barley, and will seem familiar to nearly everyone who has been on a diet. As with the oatcakes of Scotland and Ireland, once flatbrød is cooked it lasts a very long time, even years. This was a traditional necessity in mountainous Norway, where the geography and climate made agriculture and transport difficult for much of the year. Although eaten daily, breads such as this would be made only a few times annually.

MAKES 6–8

50g/2oz barley flour, plus extra for dusting
50g/2oz rye flour
50g/2oz fine oatmeal
¼ tsp salt
125–150ml/4fl oz–¼ pint water

Combine the barley flour, rye flour, oatmeal and salt in a large bowl. Make a well in the centre and gradually add the water, using only just enough to make a workable but sticky dough.

Dust a work surface with flour and briefly knead the dough into a smooth ball. Divide it into 6–8 pieces depending on the size of your griddle or frying pan.

Place a griddle or large, heavy frying pan over a medium to low heat and leave until very hot.

Roll out each piece of dough very thinly into a large circle. Trim the edges to neaten if desired. Place a circle of dough on the griddle or in the pan and cook very slowly for several minutes until quite crisp on the bottom, then turn over and cook the other side. Press down on the flatbrød with a fish slice if necessary to keep it flat against the hot surface. Reduce the heat if the bread seems to be browning rather than crisping.

Remove from the griddle or pan and repeat with the remaining rounds of dough. Eat warm or leave to cool and store in an airtight tin.

COOK'S NOTES

- Milk can be used in place of water.
- Another typical recipe features wholemeal wheat flour in place of the fine oatmeal. You could of course use spelt or Kamut flour. Other Norwegian flatbrøds include mashed potato.
- The rolled mixture can be cut into pieces and baked on a baking tray at 180°C/350°F/Gas 4 until crisp if preferred.
- When rolling the dough, remember the thinner the better to achieve the right texture.

SUMMER MINESTRONE

London's most esteemed Italian chef, Giorgio Locatelli, recommends this light and fragrant combination of borlotti beans, pancetta, truffle and farro as a warm weather soup and accordingly insists on fresh borlotti when making it. The proportions of ingredients given here are my own and can be adjusted as you prefer. A caveat from Giorgio, however, is not to use truffle oil if you have no black summer truffle. The best substitute for the real thing is truffle-flavoured pasta, which is readily available from Italian delicatessens and other gourmet shops.

SERVES 4

a little chopped pork fat, dripping or lard
1 small onion, finely chopped
250g/8oz pancetta, diced
50g/2oz farro or spelt
2 cloves garlic, finely chopped
1.5 litres/2½ pints chicken stock
1 bay leaf
1 sprig of rosemary
400g/13oz fresh borlotti beans
about 30–60g/1–2½oz leftover cooked pasta
salt and pepper
shavings of black summer truffle (optional)
rosemary, finely chopped, to serve

Heat the pork fat, dripping or lard in a large saucepan. Add the onion and cook over a low heat until translucent, stirring frequently. Add the pancetta, farro and garlic, and cook for 2–3 minutes, stirring.

Pour in the stock and add the bay and rosemary sprig. Bring to the boil, then reduce the heat and simmer gently for 30 minutes. Add the borlotti beans and continue cooking gently for a further 20 minutes or until the grains and beans are tender.

Stir the leftover cooked pasta into the soup and allow it to heat through briefly. Season to taste with salt and pepper, and serve the soup topped with shavings of black summer truffle, if available, or fresh rosemary.

COOK'S NOTES

✤ No fresh borlotti? This soup is also delicious made with broad beans, which are usually easier to find in shops and markets. Dried or canned borlotti can be substituted, but this does rather detract from the dish's summery theme.

✤ Giorgio prefers to serve this soup as a broth, but you can purée a portion of the mixture using a mouli-legumes or blender to give a thicker texture.

✤ Being rather lazy about presoaking grains, I am inclined to choose *semi-perlato* (semi-pearled) farro and simply cook it in the stock until tender. If you are using wholegrains, it is best to soak them overnight before adding to the soup.

✤ Other grains of the wheat family, such as Kamut or regular whole wheatberries, can be used here. Pearled spelt, Pasta Wheat and similar products are not suitable; they don't provide the distinctive grain taste or pleasing burst in the mouth that an unhulled or semi-perlato grain offers, and their texture is too much like that of pasta, which is also featured in the soup.

MILLET CONGEE

One of the nicest things about being in the Orient is the opportunity to enjoy traditional breakfast dishes, of which congee is one. Usually it is made from rice, although millet congee is popular in Beijing and Taiwan, where it is also a street food snack. Congee requires time to cook but very little effort – just an occasional check to ensure the pan hasn't boiled dry; if it has, simply add more water from the kettle. Congee and its Japanese cousins, zōsui and okayu, make a great, healthy late breakfast for those of us who work from home.

SERVES 2-3

100g/3½oz millet
575ml/18fl oz chicken stock
a few chopped pickled chillies
a little chopped spring onion
a few drops of soy sauce
a few drops of sesame oil
a few coriander leaves

Place the millet in a large, heavy saucepan over a moderate heat and toast the grains lightly for 1–2 minutes, stirring constantly.

Pour in the stock and bring to the boil. Half-cover the saucepan, then reduce the heat and cook gently for 1–2 hours, stirring occasionally, until the mixture has thickened and the grains have burst. Add more stock or some hot water from the kettle if the congee seems to be reducing too quickly.

Serve the congee in large bowls, sprinkled with the chopped chillies, spring onions, soy sauce, sesame oil and coriander leaves (plus any of your preferred optional extras) to taste.

COOK'S NOTES

❋ Millet gives congee a pale yellow colour and vaguely crunchy texture. You can use this basic method to make a white rice congee as well. Cooked for the same length of time, it will have a smoother and even more soothing texture than the millet version above and a slightly milder flavour.

❋ As with other porridge dishes, the correct serving consistency is the one that you prefer.

❋ Optional extras to stir into the congee shortly before serving include slices of char siu (Chinese barbecue roast pork), which can be bought ready-cooked from Chinese stores, some cooked chicken or prawns, salted peanuts or a little grated fresh root ginger. Sprinkle in a few drops of fish sauce if you like it. I often add some green veg too, such as pak choy, putting the sliced stems in the congee a few minutes before the leaves.

❋ Don't try and use any of the Chinese coloured rices for congee – when cooked to a pulp, they look highly unappetizing.

❋ White rice and corn is a fabulous combination and I love Edward Lee's recipe for creamed corn and mushroom congee in his book *Smoke & Pickles*. Unusually he stirs an egg plus some lemon juice and zest into the pan just before serving.

❋ From time to time I also make an Indian version that involves frying mustard seeds, ground turmeric, asafoetida, ginger, cumin and coriander together in ghee before adding 2 parts white basmati rice, 1 part split yellow mung beans and 10 parts water. The mixture needs to simmer for a good hour. Add fresh coriander just before serving.

❋ Australian food writer Jill Dupleix makes the excellent suggestion of serving congee as a late supper dish with a glass of Champagne.

CORN STOCK

I love the frugality of this recipe. It follows the admirable tradition of many of the world's poorer countries of making effective use of every part of the plant, or animal. Mexicans certainly put all parts of the maize plant to work, though not in this particular way. Simmered long enough, leftover sweetcorn cobs produce an interesting, intensely flavoured alternative to shellfish stock. When cooked for a shorter time, they make a good light vegetable stock, adding welcome diversity to the range of tastes available to vegetarians for soups, sauces and stews.

MAKES 600ML/1 PINT

4–6 leftover sweetcorn cobs
   (kernels removed)
1.6 litres/2½ pints water
1 small onion, halved
1 carrot, scraped
½ celery stick
10 peppercorns
1–2 bay leaves
2 sprigs of thyme
salt

Using a meat cleaver or large cook's knife, chop each sweetcorn cob into 4 pieces. They can be a bit tough, so if you don't manage to cut right the way through the cob, don't worry; once a cut is made, the cob will easily snap into two.

Place the chopped cobs in a stockpot with the water. Add the onion, carrot, celery, peppercorns, bay, thyme and a little salt, and bring to the boil. Half-cover the pot, reduce the heat and simmer very gently for 2 hours.

Strain the stock, pressing down on the solids to extract as much flavour as possible. Use as it is or place in a clean saucepan and boil rapidly over a high heat until the stock has reduced and its flavour has intensified to your liking.

COOK'S NOTES

❉ The recipe here might be called traditional in terms of its flavourings, but variations of it are in no way restricted to these aromatics, or indeed this method.
❉ Chef Douglas Rodriguez (see page 52) includes leeks, saffron, jalapeno chillies and tomato paste in his version, sweating the vegetables and saffron in butter before adding the water and other herbs and spices.
❉ Joseph Sponzo (see page 60) uses some of the kernels from the sweetcorn cobs and includes only basil stems and tarragon sprigs as flavourings. He adds the herbs once the stock has been reduced and removed from the heat, and discards them before storing or further cooking. This infusion method of flavouring is favoured by some meticulous chefs who argue that boiling herbs over an extended period causes bitterness in the finished stock.
❉ To make a roasted corn stock, spray the pieces of cob with oil and roast for 30 minutes at 200°C/400°F/ Gas 6, then sprinkle half a chopped onion over the cobs and continue roasting for another 10 minutes or so. Tip the lot into a pot, add plenty of water and simmer for 1 hour before straining.

QUINOA, CHICKEN AND SPINACH SOUP

Chef Douglas Rodriguez is one of my favourite restaurateurs and food writers, primarily because his inspirational 'Nuevo Latino' style combines both common and exotic ingredients using unfamiliar but generally simple techniques. This recipe is based on one in his book *Latin Ladles*, and treats quinoa as it needs to be treated, with the sweetness of the chicken stock, chillies and herbs off-setting the natural bitterness of the grain. It's great 'flu' food and, although the taste and texture change slightly in the freezer, good to make and store.

SERVES 6–8

1 medium whole chicken
2 litres/3½ pints water
2 onions
3 celery sticks
2 carrots, roughly chopped
1 bouquet garni
5–7 garlic cloves
a large bunch of coriander
6 sprigs of parsley
3 tbsp butter, softened
500g/1lb baby spinach leaves
leaves from 6 sprigs of mint
3 jalapeno chillies, finely chopped
150g/5oz quinoa, rinsed thoroughly
5 spring onions, finely chopped
salt and pepper

Rinse the chicken and place it in a large stockpot with the measured water. Halve one onion and roughly chop 2 celery sticks and add them to the pot, together with the carrots, bouquet garni, 4 unpeeled garlic cloves and the stalks from the coriander and parsley.

Bring to the boil, then half-cover the pot, reduce the heat right down and simmer for 1 hour or until the chicken is done.

Carefully lift out the cooked chicken, allowing the liquid in the cavity to run back into the pot. Set the chicken aside to cool. Strain the stock, discarding the solids, and rinse out the pot.

Finely chop the remaining onion, celery and garlic. Melt the butter in the stockpot, add the chopped vegetables and sauté gently for 5 minutes. Add the spinach, coriander, parsley and mint leaves, plus the chillies, and cook for another 3–5 minutes.

Pour in the stock and bring it to the boil. Add the rinsed quinoa and spring onions. Reduce the heat, then half-cover the pot and simmer for 30 minutes. Add some hot water to the soup if it is reducing rapidly.

Meanwhile, remove the chicken meat from the bones and shred into bite-sized pieces. When the soup has been cooking for 30 minutes, stir in the chicken and allow it to heat through. Season to taste with salt and pepper before serving.

COOK'S NOTES

- White rice or hominy are good alternatives to quinoa in this soup.
- For a quicker version of this recipe, use ready-made stock and 4–5 chicken thighs. Cook them in the stock for 20–25 minutes with the herb stalks before picking up the recipe at the point where the vegetables are sautéed.
- I like to add some finely sliced red chillies to this soup for their attractive colour contrast.

PERSIAN-STYLE BARLEY SOUP

Actually, this type of barley soup is not strictly Persian, merely popular in Tehran, according to the late Margaret Shaida who lived in Iran for 25 years and learned to cook its traditional dishes from her Persian mother-in-law. In her book *The Legendary Cuisine of Persia*, Margaret theorizes that this soup entered Iran only in the early part of the 20th century, thanks to the White Russians fleeing the Bolshevik Revolution. This version differs from hers only in so far as it incorporates my own (often lazy) culinary habits and aversion to grating.

SERVES 4

2 tbsp olive oil

2 onions, finely chopped

2 leeks, finely chopped

2 carrots, finely chopped

150g/5oz semi-pearled or pot barley

1.5 litres/2½ pints lamb stock

juice of 2 lemons

2 tbsp soured cream

a handful of chopped parsley

salt and pepper

In a large, heavy saucepan, heat the olive oil and gently fry the onion until translucent. Add the leeks and carrots and continue frying gently until softened.

Add the barley and stock and bring to the boil. Half-cover the pan, reduce the heat and simmer for 1½–2 hours, stirring occasionally to prevent sticking, until the mixture is thick and the ingredients are breaking down. Add more stock or some hot water from the kettle if it reduces too quickly.

Pour half the lemon juice into the saucepan and continue cooking until the barley is soft. Remove from the heat and stir in the soured cream and most of the parsley, adding the remaining lemon juice to taste. Season to taste with salt and pepper, and serve sprinkled with the reserved parsley.

COOK'S NOTES

✣ Margaret's recipe uses pearl barley, and slightly more of it. I prefer the taste of pot barley and, wanting to keep only one variety in the cupboard, would use it in preference.

✣ The traditional Persian way of incorporating the carrot is to grate it and add it along with the lemon juice, after the soup has been cooking for some time.

✣ Barley goes particularly well with lamb stock, but there is no reason why beef, chicken or a richly flavoured vegetable stock could not be used instead.

✣ The wheat family of grains make a good alternative to barley especially in this soup.

✣ For a barley soup in the German style, sauté some leeks and celery in butter, then add about half the quantity of barley used here and your choice of chicken or veal stock. Skip the lemon juice and soured cream, seasoning instead with nutmeg. To thicken the soup, make a 'liaison' of 120ml/4fl oz cream beaten together with an egg yolk and slowly stir the hot soup into it. A garnish of parsley is optional.

SORGHUM CHICKEN SALAD WITH COCONUT AND LIME

Sorghum is unusual in being a mild grain that is very chewy (it's a wonder the Americans don't call it sorghum berries), so this slow, flavour-absorbing cooking technique suits it perfectly. The chilli is slit, rather than halved or sliced, to give a wonderfully warming background heat without making the dish too fiery. This salad is perfect made with the remains of a chicken roasted a day or two before, and the quantities can easily be doubled or trebled to feed more.

SERVES 2

100g/3½oz sorghum

2 large slices of fresh root ginger

1 green chilli, slit lengthways at the tip

1–2 coriander roots, bashed, or handful of coriander stalks

150–200g/5–7oz leftover roast chicken

15g/½oz coriander leaves

3 tbsp mint leaves

a handful of large basil leaves, or to taste

10 cherry tomatoes, halved

30g/1¼oz baby spinach leaves

50ml/2fl oz coconut cream

50ml/2fl oz lime juice

salt and pepper

Put the sorghum in a saucepan with the ginger, chilli and coriander roots. Cover generously with water and bring to the boil. Reduce the heat to a slow simmer and cook for 1 hour, testing at 50 minutes to see if the grains are al dente. Top up with hot water from the kettle if the water level falls below the surface of the grains during cooking.

Drain the sorghum in a large sieve and rinse under cold running water. Remove and discard the ginger, chilli and coriander roots or stalks. Set aside the sorghum to drain and cool completely.

Use your hands to break the chicken into bite-sized pieces (this looks much better than using a knife), then tear up the herbs leaves, keeping the basil separate.

Combine the sorghum, chicken, coriander and mint in a salad bowl. Add the cherry tomatoes and spinach leaves and toss. Stir together the coconut cream and lime juice and pour over the salad. Season well with salt and pepper and toss again. Scatter with the basil leaves before serving.

COOK'S NOTES

❉ The first time I made this salad I used leftover Christmas turkey, which was perfect. It's just the sort of punchy, easygoing yet healthful dish you want to eat post-holiday feast. It would also be great with leftover roast beef.

❉ You could give it a Thai slant by adding a bruised lemongrass stalk and a crumpled kaffir lime leaf to the cooking water.

❉ Even if you double the quantity of sorghum, there is no need to increase the quantities of flavourings in the cooking water.

❉ Use quinoa, millet or wholegrain rice in place of sorghum if preferred, but reduce the cooking times accordingly (see pages 184–5).

BROWN RICE AND CHIA LUNCH BOWL

The idea for this 'power lunch' came from Feng Sushi founder Silla Bjerrum; the original version is in her book *Simple Japanese*. The formula is easy: grain, a little protein, blanched or wilted greens, some raw vegetables, plus herbs and sauces or condiments. The cooked grain can be kept covered in the fridge for a few days, providing the base for a couple of quick lunches.

SERVES 3-4

For the rice base

150g/5oz whole short-grain rice

440ml/¾ pint water

1 tsp sugar

1–2 tbsp Japanese rice vinegar, or more to taste

2 tsp olive or sesame oil

1 tbsp chia seeds

20 chives, finely chopped

salt and pepper

For the topping

20g/¾oz dried wakame

300g/10oz frozen edamame or broad beans

150g/5oz asparagus tips

1 carrot

300g/10oz hot-smoked or kiln-roast salmon

a small handful of coriander leaves

4–8 shiso leaves

To serve

wasabi-flavoured furikake

soy sauce

Wash and drain the rice and put it in a saucepan with the measured water. Bring to the boil, then reduce to a very low heat, cover and cook for 30 minutes. Turn the heat off under the pan and leave the rice to steam in the residual heat for a further 20 minutes.

Transfer the cooked rice to a bowl. Dissolve the sugar and a pinch of salt in the rice vinegar, then stir it into the rice along with the oil, chia seeds and chives. Adjust the seasoning with more vinegar, oil and/or salt and pepper according to taste. Set aside to cool.

Bring a saucepan of water to the boil. Put the wakame in a heatproof bowl and carefully ladle some of the boiling water over it. Set aside to rehydrate for 10 minutes. Meanwhile, blanch the beans and asparagus tips separately in the saucepan – for 3 minutes and 1 minute respectively. Drain and refresh under cold running water, then set aside.

Finely grate the carrot, using a Japanese turner if you have one. Peel the beans. Drain the wakame and pat dry with kitchen paper. Break the salmon into bite-sized pieces.

Scoop the rice mixture into serving bowls and arrange the beans, asparagus, salmon, carrot and herbs on top. Sprinkle with furikake and soy sauce before serving.

COOK'S NOTES

❉ Swap the ingredients to suit your taste and what you have in the cupboard. Canned tuna and salmon work well for a simple supper. I enjoy the combination of smoked salmon with boiled egg, cucumber and avocado. Ikura (salmon roe) is a low-prep Japanese ingredient that looks very pretty here. For a change you could replace the soy sauce with a ready-made Japanese-y salad dressing.

❉ This rice mixture can be used to make sushi rolls. Traditional sushi rice contains rather more vinegar (use up to 3 tbsp and increase the sugar to 1 tbsp) and no oil.

❉ Silla uses brown basmati rice for this mixture and it has the advantage of cooking more quickly than short grain. If you want to shape the mixture into maki rolls, it is worth buying brown sushi rice, which is shorter, fatter and stickier, but be careful not to let it overcook, as it readily turns into a soggy mess.

❉ Replace the chia seeds with poppy seeds (Silla's choice) or toasted sesame seeds, if you prefer, and swap the carrot for other root vegetables such as beetroot or mooli (daikon).

SPONZO SALAD

Just as he was leaving to spend the summer working in Florence, private chef Joseph Sponzo thrust a scrawled recipe into my hand to test. I was naturally hoping for something chocolate, so my heart sank when I read the title 'Millet and Aduki Bean Salad'. How uninspiring. Yet the fresh herbs, vegetables and tangy cheese he matched with grains elevated them into a superb dish. Here it's been simplified considerably into a good midweek supper for summer.

SERVES 2

50g/2oz dried aduki beans

75g/3oz millet

60g/2½oz broad beans

50g/2oz red chard stems, chopped

50g/2oz fresh peas

6 sun-dried tomatoes preserved in oil,
    or semi-dried or roast tomatoes, chopped,
    plus 3–4 tbsp oil from the tomatoes

2 spring onions, chopped

15g/½oz unpacked mixed herb leaves such as
    basil, dill, chervil, oregano, parsley, rocket

1 tbsp olive oil, or herb- or garlic-flavoured oil

1½ tbsp red wine vinegar or balsamic vinegar

25g/1oz Parmesan, pecorino or hard sheep's
    milk cheese such as Duddleswell, shaved

salt and pepper

Bring a large saucepan of water to the boil and add the aduki beans. Simmer for 45–60 minutes or until the beans are almost tender. About 10 minutes before the end of cooking, scatter in the millet and continue boiling until the beans and millet are done.

Meanwhile, bring another saucepan of water to the boil and add a pinch of salt. Add the broad beans and simmer for 1 minute. Remove with a slotted spoon and set aside to cool.

Add the red chard stems to the boiling water and simmer for 2 minutes. Drain under cold running water and set aside to dry. Meanwhile, peel the broad beans.

When the aduki beans and millet are cooked, drain them well under cold running water and leave to drain and cool.

In a large bowl combine the broad beans, red chard stems, the uncooked peas, tomatoes, spring onions, herb leaves, aduki beans and millet. Toss to combine, then pour in the oil from the tomatoes, plus the other oil, and the vinegar. Season thoroughly with salt and pepper. Just before serving, toss in the cheese.

COOK'S NOTES

✻ Although I'm reluctant to fiddle with the base of aduki and millet, there is plenty of room for variation in this salad, including replacing the cheese with flakes of honey-roast salmon, which can be bought ready-made from the supermarket, and using artichokes or asparagus instead of the broad beans.

✻ To accompany the salad, though it is actually a meal in itself, you could lay fillets of grilled chicken or roast salmon on top, or kebabs of grilled prawns or beef (see page 160).

✻ When preparing this for a dinner party or buffet, consider cooking the millet and aduki separately, so that the millet doesn't take on a pink tinge. Or use canned aduki, which would cut the overall cooking time considerably.

✻ Joseph had access to a wide variety of fresh organic produce. If you do too, add nasturtium leaves and fennel fronds to the mixed herb selection, as Joseph did in his original.

✻ The chard stems provide crunch and colour as well as a slightly acidic flavour. If red chard is unavailable, try replacing it with radishes or chopped deseeded Lebanese cucumber.

✻ Chard leaves are often cooked separately from their stalks, which, in the South of France, are served tossed with butter and lemon, while the leaves might be fed to animals. The leaves can be easily used in other dishes, such as African Corn and Peanut Patties (page 123) and Quinoa, Chicken and Spinach Soup (page 52). If the leaves are young, they can be used in salads, like baby spinach.

RICE AND RICOTTA SALAD

If wholegrain rice salad makes you think of macramé and sandals, this simple, bright-tasting combination will change your perceptions. It is based on a hot rice dish by Viana La Place, author of the wonderful *Verdura: Vegetables Italian Style* and several other inspiring cookbooks. Ricotta is perhaps the most useful cheese for cooking, yet being made from whey (a by-product of cheesemaking), it is technically not cheese at all. Some ricottas are smooth and creamy, some a little more granular, others aged until hard. Use a soft, fresh style here.

SERVES 2

75g/3oz ricotta
2 tbsp chopped mixed herbs such as basil,
    marjoram or oregano, parsley and rocket
a little finely grated lemon zest, to taste
100g/3½oz wholegrain or semi-pearled rice
salt and pepper

Combine the ricotta, herbs, lemon zest and some salt and pepper in a small mixing bowl and set aside.

Bring a large pan of lightly salted water to the boil. Add the rice and simmer for 20–25 minutes or until the grains are tender. Drain the rice, rinse briefly and drain again thoroughly.

Add the still-warm rice to the flavoured ricotta and toss to combine. Adjust the seasonings to taste and serve at warm room temperature.

COOK'S NOTES

✣ Choose brown rice if you like, but red or black tend to look more interesting on the plate. Be sure to rinse and drain coloured rices well, so that the brightly coloured cooking liquid doesn't run into the ricotta.

✣ Wild rice (the colour of which doesn't run) is another option for this recipe.

✣ Serve this on its own, perhaps with a green or tomato salad, as a light meal, or with grilled chicken (see page 160) for something more substantial. It's also good featured as part of a mezze-style selection of little dishes.

✣ Viana La Place's unusual original recipe features white arborio rice boiled in a generous quantity of salted water, rather than stir-cooked as for risotto. She also includes butter and Parmesan cheese, which are unnecessary in the context of a cool salad, the butter in particular making it a little too rich and heavy for serving at room temperature.

HAZELNUT AND FETA SPROUT SALAD

Really good sprout salads are a rare thing. I've looked around but eaten only a couple worth writing about – one an elegant little pile of virtue prepared by chef Stephen Bull several years ago when he had a restaurant in the City of London. This dish is based on it. Success lies not in the sprouts but the ingredients chosen to match them. You don't often see cheese in a sprout salad, but as a little of what we fancy does us good, and helps the sprouts to do us good, what's the problem? Buy ewes' milk feta if you have a problem with cows' milk.

SERVES 4

150g/5oz hazelnuts

2 oranges

5cm/2in piece of cucumber, finely chopped

1–2 celery sticks, finely chopped

75g/3oz buckwheat sprouts

75g/3oz short mung bean or lentil sprouts

20g/¾oz alfalfa sprouts

150g/5oz feta cheese, crumbled

2 tbsp hazelnut oil

1 tsp Dijon mustard

flat-leaf parsley or salad cress, to garnish

salt and pepper

Heat the oven to 200°C/400°F/Gas 6. Place the hazelnuts on a small baking tray and roast for about 20 minutes, shaking the pan frequently, until the skins are blackened. Remove from the oven and wrap the nuts in a clean tea towel. Set aside to cool.

Remove the peel and pith from 1 of the oranges. Holding it over a mixing bowl, use a serrated fruit knife to cut the segments of orange flesh from the connective tissue and let them fall into the bowl, collecting as much of the juice as possible.

Toss the chopped cucumber and celery into the bowl and set aside. Use the tea towel to help rub the charred skins away from the roasted hazelnuts. Discard the skins and chop the nuts in half, or more roughly if preferred. Add to the bowl with the sprouts and crumbled cheese, and toss well.

Juice the remaining orange and place in a small bowl with the nut oil and mustard. Whisk together, then season to taste with salt and pepper.

Stir the dressing into the salad and adjust the seasoning as necessary (the feta will be very salty). Serve on plates garnished with small sprigs of flat-leaf parsley or a few strands of cress, as desired.

COOK'S NOTES

✽ Despite what some health faddists may think, there is such a thing as too many sprouts. The quantities here are just a starting point. Adjust the amount of each ingredient to suit your own taste. You want to feel the salad is so delicious that you'd like to make it again one day, not that if you took just one more mouthful you'd turn into a horse.

✽ Large Chinese-style mung bean sprouts are not ideal but are an acceptable inclusion. Before adding them to the salad, blanch for 1 minute in a large pan of boiling water, refresh under cold running water and dry thoroughly.

✽ This is a complete meal in itself, a fine lunchbox dish or a good winter side salad for plainly grilled lamb or chicken (see page 160).

BARLEY AND YOGURT SALAD

Yogurt is thought to have originated in Central Asia, although its use as an ingredient has spread widely and become traditional in many diverse cuisines. This North African recipe was given to food writer Marlena Spieler while she was working on a dude ranch in the Galilee, Israel. 'Like all of my favourite dishes, the garlic taste comes through loud and clear,' she says. It differs from similar yogurt salads in that it features grain rather than chopped vegetables. Agnar Sverrison, who hails from Iceland, serves a similar combination as a dip at his restaurant Texture.

SERVES 4

150g/5oz pot barley

150g/5oz Greek-style or other thick
    and creamy yogurt

2 garlic cloves, crushed

juice of ½ lemon, or more to taste

1 spring onion, finely sliced

a few sprigs of herbs such as oregano,
    marjoram, mint or parsley

salt and pepper

Place the barley in the small grinding bowl of a food processor or an electric coffee mill and pulse briefly to crack the grains.

Transfer the barley to a small saucepan, cover with a generous quantity of water and bring to the boil. Reduce the heat and simmer until the barley is tender.

Drain the cooked barley, rinse it under cold running water and drain again thoroughly.

In a mixing bowl, combine the barley, yogurt, garlic and lemon juice, stirring well. Season to taste with salt and pepper, adding extra lemon juice if desired. Serve topped with the spring onion and herb leaves, chopped if preferred.

COOK'S NOTES

* The quality of the garlic is all important here because it will be eaten raw. If the cloves are strong and bitter, don't use them.
* A scaled-down version of this salad is a good way of employing leftover cooked grains. Keep them whole if you like, or roughly chop them before stirring into the yogurt.
* Agnar's recipe combines plain natural and Greek yogurts, pearl barley, plus chives, dill, mint, parsley, lemon zest and a little sugar. No garlic.
* Warm seeded flatbread is the tastiest accompaniment, as well as any Middle Eastern vegetable salad dishes, or simply crudités and herbs. The key is to choose items that offer textural contrast to the creamy dip.
* For a Lebanese-style yogurt salad, replace the barley with chopped cucumber, leave out the lemon, spring onion and fresh herbs, and flavour instead with a little dried mint. This is also reminiscent of Indian raita, which might feature fresh coriander, green chilli and ginger as flavourings, as well as tomato.
* The Tamils of Southern India combine rice and yogurt in a summery salad. It's slightly more involved than the quick dip given here. To make it, you need to fry ½ tsp mustard seeds in a little vegetable oil with a few curry leaves, a dried red chilli and some finely chopped fresh root ginger. Tip this over boiled and drained basmati rice, then stir in a similar volume of yogurt that you have whisked together with a little milk and salt. Serve the 'curd rice' topped with finely sliced green chillies and a piquant Indian pickle.

SPROUTS

To be honest, I really do think beans, lentils and large seeds are easier to sprout than cereal grains. The process is simple in theory, but in practice good results depend very much on the quality of grains you buy. It is imperative to purchase from a store that specializes in grains for sprouting rather than for cooking. Sprouting is fun to do if you have children in the house, as they take such delight in the growing process.

MAKES ABOUT 125ML/4FL OZ

2 tbsp grains or seeds for sprouting

Choose a fairly tall, wide-bottomed and large-mouthed jar. Cut a piece of loosely woven muslin or mesh cloth large enough to fit over the top of the jar and down the sides, so that it can be secured with an elastic band at the neck.

Decide how you are going to place the jar in your kitchen so that it can stand upside down at an angle for a few hours after each rinsing to encourage all water to drain away.

Place the grains in a bowl of fresh water and agitate them gently with your hand so that any broken grains and 'floaters' make themselves known to you. Discard them.

Drain the grains and return them to the bowl, adding plenty of fresh water. Leave to soak for the required time (see page 188).

After this initial soaking, drain the grains again and transfer to the jar. Rinse the grains 3 times a day for around 3 days or until they have grown sprouts 5mm–1cm/¼–½ in long.

Pat dry with kitchen paper, peel any loose husks away if desired and discard any unsprouted grains. Place the sprouts in a clean dry jar, store in the fridge and use within 3–7 days.

COOK'S NOTES

❖ Buckwheat sprouts are fast and easy, so if you haven't done any sprouting since school, start with them. The right grains are easy to spot: they have a rough, chocolate-brown shell. Chia are good too but are best sprouted with the seeds spread on a plate or tray rather than in a jar.

❖ Unfortunately, sorghum is not suitable for sprouting at home.

❖ Stacks of sprouting trays work well, but don't purchase one until you have used the jar method a few times and decided sprouting is really for you.

❖ The other key ingredient is a routine, so that rinsing becomes almost a mindless action rather than something that is easy to forget. If the grains need to be rinsed 3 times a day, the best schedule is to do it before work, after work and before bed.

❖ Poor drainage is the fast-track to mouldy, smelly sprouts. One way to maximize drainage is to sit the upturned jar on a dish drainer over the kitchen sink, or even better a tray or bowl.

❖ The soaking water is considered to be very nutritious. If you don't want to drink it, give it to your plants.

❖ The ideal sprouting temperature is 17–24°C/63–75°F. Sprouts are essentially a springtime food. If it's a hot summer, expect to have problems with germination and fermentation.

❖ The best way to use sprouts is very sparingly. Sprinkle just a tiny amount over a green salad, then remove half of them before serving.

QUINOA, CASHEW AND GRAPE SALAD

Lyn Hall, whom chef Michel Roux Senior of The Waterside Inn has described as 'the best of all cookery teachers', has devised what may be one of the best modern uses of quinoa. Fruit vinegar is an excellent foil for the natural bitterness of the grain and, for me at least, this salad has proved a welcome way to use up the raspberry vinegar that has been sitting in the kitchen since 1989, when it was fashionable. Like many grain salads, this is ideal for the buffet table, as it can stand for several hours without deteriorating.

SERVES 2

150g/5oz quinoa
60g/2½oz raw cashew nuts
2 tbsp raspberry or apple cider vinegar
1 tbsp mirin
2 tsp chopped herbs such as rocket, mint, marjoram or dill
1 celery stick, finely sliced
100g/3½oz seedless grapes, halved
salt and pepper

Bring a large pan of lightly salted water to the boil. Add the quinoa and simmer for 12–15 minutes or until the grains are tender and the equatorial threads detached. Drain, rinse and drain again thoroughly. Spread the quinoa out on a baking tray to dry.

In a dry, heavy frying pan, toast the cashews over a moderate to low heat, stirring frequently, until they are golden brown. Remove to a bowl to cool, then chop them roughly.

In a large bowl, combine the vinegar, mirin and ¼ tsp salt. Toss in the herbs, then add the celery, grapes, cooked quinoa and cashews.

Adjust the seasoning to taste and leave the salad to stand for at least 1 hour before serving.

COOK'S NOTES

✻ The quinoa can be cooked in vegetable or chicken stock instead of water for a more complex flavour.
✻ Wild rice or unhulled black, brown or red rice are good alternatives to quinoa, in which case hazelnuts or almonds could also be used in place of the cashews.
✻ Lyn uses red grapes for her salad, but green grapes, or a mixture of the two, are equally attractive.
✻ Stores permitting, I'm inclined to use basil, coriander and lime juice in place of vinegar and mirin.
✻ Lyn recommends a hearty vegetable soup and bean dish to turn it into a full meal. Grilled chicken, fish or prawns (see pages 160–1) and a green salad are other good possibilities.
✻ Fruit and grain is, in general, a good salad combination that's worth exploring using these basic proportions as a guide. Farro, Parma ham and dried apricots work well. An idea from Home Restaurant in Greenwich Village, New York is to combine wild rice and barley with fresh blackberries and herbs.

BARLEY GRIT COUSCOUS

Many people don't realize that couscous is a product (and dish) made from grains, not a grain itself. And while wheat is the most common type of couscous, it is authentically made with various grains including barley, corn, millet, green wheat and sorghum. Explore a top-notch health food shop these days and you may find several of these on offer. I admit that since having a child I am less pedantic about steaming and rubbing couscous (as opposed to simply letting it hydrate in boiling water).

SERVES 2

150g/5oz barley grits, or uncracked semi-pearled or pot barley, or barley couscous

2 tbsp olive oil

1 onion, sliced or chopped

1 garlic clove, chopped or crushed

400g/13oz canned chopped tomatoes

a large pinch of powdered saffron

600ml/1 pint water

1 tsp butter, plus extra for greasing

6 tbsp water

200g/7oz firm fish such as marlin, cubed

a large handful of basil, torn

salt and pepper

COOK'S NOTES

❉ Barley grit couscous is a favourite with North African Berbers, though the stew I've given here is not an authentic recipe. To make it a vegetarian dish, replace the fish with cauliflower florets, cut small, and add to the sauce just 2–3 minutes before serving.

❉ Now that Belazu barley couscous is readily available, I tend to keep a pack in the cupboard as norm rather than cracking the barley myself, though I do enjoy the more rugged texture that results from using that method. You could also use cracked freekeh in this recipe.

❉ Millet couscous pellets, typical of African cooking, are easy to make, but freshly ground flour is essential, otherwise the dish will have an unpleasant bitter aftertaste. You simply place the millet flour in a bowl and gradually work in water, rubbing the flour together with your fingers and raking through it until tiny balls are achieved.

If using uncracked barley, place it in the bowl of the grinding attachment of a food processor and pulse until the grains are cracked but not finely ground. Place the barley grits, cracked barley or couscous in a large bowl and cover with water. Set aside to soak.

Meanwhile, heat the oil in the base of the couscousiere or steamer, add the onion and garlic and fry gently until tender. Add the tomatoes, saffron and water and bring to the boil, then reduce the heat to low.

Arrange the top part of the couscousiere, or a steamer basket lined with buttered muslin, over the pan. Squeeze the excess water from the grits and add them gradually to the top section, rubbing them between your palms as you drop them in. Cover and leave to cook for 20 minutes.

Remove the top section of the pot from the heat and dump the grits into a large bowl or roasting tray. Break the lumps up with a fork and stir in the butter. Gradually sprinkle the water over the grain, raking it in with the fork.

Stir the tomato sauce well, then return the barley to the steamer and place over the pan. Steam for a further 20 minutes. Remove the grain from the steamer and fork through again.

When the tomato sauce has thickened considerably, add the fish, basil and salt and pepper. Return the grain to the steamer, place back over the stew and steam for a further 10–15 minutes or until the fish is cooked and the barley grits are tender.

Fluff up the barley again and place in warm serving bowls. Adjust the seasoning of the fish stew to taste, spoon it over the barley and serve.

SPAGHETTI WITH SARDINES AND FENNEL

Please don't dismiss wholewheat pasta because you tried it once and thought it awful. Some brands will never cook to the correct al dente texture. Look for authentic Italian manufacturers using artisan methods, such as La Terra e il Cielo. I'm particular about the shape too: thin types such as spaghetti and linguine wholewheat pasta give the best mouthfeel though I accept that if you've had children you are buying more fusilli than you ever thought possible.

SERVES 2

4 fillets of large fresh sardines, or 6 smaller ones
200g/7oz wholemeal wheat-type spaghetti
1 tbsp olive oil, plus extra to taste
½ fennel bulb, finely chopped
1 garlic clove, chopped
2–3 tbsp chopped flat-leaf parsley
juice of ½ lemon
salt and pepper

Pat dry the sardine fillets and sprinkle them lightly with salt. Bring a large saucepan of salted water to the boil, add the pasta and cook according to the packet instructions.

Meanwhile, heat the olive oil in a large frying pan, add the fennel and garlic and cook, stirring, for 30 seconds or until fragrant. Add the sardine fillets to the pan skin-side down. Cook for 1 minute, turn them over and cook for another minute or until done. Remove from the heat.

Drain the pasta and return it to the saucepan. Add the sardine and fennel mixture, plus the parsley, and toss, adding a little extra olive oil if desired. Season to taste with salt, pepper and lots of lemon juice.

COOK'S NOTES

✳ This southern Italian dish was a favourite of London-based chef David Eyre while working at renowned gastropub The Eagle. David's recipe differs from mine in that it doubles the quantity of sardines per person and uses more olive oil. I use more fennel instead. Even though I'm not a great fan of its aniseed flavour, it does work well in this context with lemon and parsley.

✳ As with the dish overleaf, this recipe is at its best with a very thin wholewheat pasta shape such as spaghetti or linguine.

✳ To clean, gut and fillet sardines yourself, wipe their scales away underneath cold running water and dry with kitchen towel. Press your thumb right along their backs to loosen the flesh from the spine. Using a small sharp knife, cut off and discard their heads, then cut lengthways along the bellies. Open the belly flaps and pull out and discard the innards. Press the fish open while running your thumb along one side of the spine to assist the flattening. Working from the neck ends, pull the spines out of the fish and snap them off at the tails. Separate the fillets, then rinse them clean and pat dry.

✳ The combination of wholewheat pasta and oily fish is not exclusive to southern Italy. In Venice, a traditional dish of wholewheat pasta features a sweet-sour sauce of anchovies and onions. The bigoli pasta is a long noodle but very thick, a point that may contribute to the dish's lack of popularity outside its local area.

PASTA WITH TOMATOES, OLIVES AND WALNUTS

On a hot summer's day, this cold, elegant dish is wonderfully refreshing, and a million miles closer to Italy than the anglicized pasta salads that have given cold pasta such a bad reputation. Tomato sauces generally work well with wholewheat pasta – cream, egg and thick cheese sauces tend to make less pleasing matches. If you want to avoid wheat altogether, corn/maize spaghetti is the best alternative, by some margin in my view.

PER PERSON

30g/1¼oz broken walnuts
1 medium ripe tomato
100g/3½oz wholemeal wheat-type
    linguine or spaghetti
7 marinated purple olives such as kalamata,
    stoned
1 tbsp olive oil or oil from the marinated olives
a small handful of basil leaves
salt and pepper

Put a kettle of water on to boil. Meanwhile, in a dry frying pan, lightly toast the walnuts until just fragrant, stirring constantly. Transfer to a bowl to cool.

With a small, sharp knife, score a cross in the rounded end of the tomato and place in a heatproof bowl. Pour some boiling water from the kettle over the tomato and leave for 1–2 minutes.

Pour the rest of the water from the kettle into a large saucepan. Add a little salt and bring to the boil. Cook the pasta according to the packet instructions.

Meanwhile, drain the tomato and peel away the skin. Remove the core, then quarter the tomato and remove and discard the seeds. Dice the flesh and add to the bowl with the walnuts.

Roughly chop the stoned olives and place with the tomato and nuts. When the pasta is only just al dente, drain and refresh it under cold running water. When it has thoroughly drained, toss it with the tomato, nuts and olives, adding the olive oil or some of the leftover marinating oil from the olives.

Tear the basil leaves into the pasta, season to taste with salt and pepper and then toss again before serving at room temperature.

COOK'S NOTES

✳ If you have been wondering how best to use those wholemeal spelt noodles in the health food shop, this is the dish to try. Simply scale this recipe up according to the number of people you are feeding. It works very well as a quick summer supper, lunch or appetizer.

✳ Use buckwheat noodles if preferred – the flavour is wonderful with juicy tomatoes – and add a little chilli and garlic to the sauce if desired.

✳ Like many people, I usually ignore instructions in cookbooks to skin tomatoes, but here the luscious effect of the peeled flesh is important. Given the lack of other cooking required for the dish, it does not greatly affect the preparation time or degree of effort, but the results are well worth it.

✳ Purple olives are specified merely because their colour enhances the dish. Use black olives if you prefer. If your olives are not already marinated in a lovely mixture of oil, herbs and an acidic element such as vinegar or lemon, add these ingredients to the finished dish yourself, adjusting the flavours to taste.

BUCKWHEAT NOODLES

It is a slow waltz I most remember in learning to make soba noodles from Yoshio Miyazawa in Shinjuku. His one-two-three, one-two-three rhythm of working the water into the flour was taught to him by his father, and also used when cutting the rolled dough. A special wide-bladed knife is grasped from above and lined up alongside a wooden guard to keep it straight and protect the hand. The guard is pushed along a few millimetres after each cut, then the knife is lifted ready to cut again, beating out a repetitive rhythm: cut-slide-up, cut-slide-up.

SERVES 4

300g/10oz buckwheat flour,
    plus extra for dusting
a little water, to mix
salt

COOK'S NOTES

✳ Serve the noodles cold with the Japanese dipping sauce on page 81. Top with freshly toasted nori seaweed cut into fine strips with scissors, and add some finely chopped spring onion to the sauce if desired.

✳ You can use soba noodles to make Korean dishes (however, strictly speaking, Korea's buckwheat noodle naeng myun is a different product and hard to make at home as it contains sweet potato starch). So for a Korean flavour, toss the noodles with chilli sauce (see page 162), garnish with hard-boiled egg, sliced boiled beef and finely grated Korean radish, tong chimi or mooli. Add cucumber if desired.

✳ The Italian buckwheat noodle, pizzoccheri, is cut wider than soba. A classic combination is to combine it with boiled potato and cabbage. Make a sauce by frying in butter half a finely chopped onion with 2 torn sage leaves and a little chopped garlic. Toss the sauce, noodles and vegetables with 50g/2oz diced fontina and 25g/1oz Parmesan, then bake covered at 180°C/350°F/Gas 4 for 5 minutes so that the cheese melts.

✳ Another easy Italian way with buckwheat noodles is to toss them with a sauce of wild mushrooms (see page 162).

Place the flour in a large, wide mixing bowl and make a well in the centre. Pour in about 1 tbsp water and, using your hand like a claw, gradually work a little of the flour into the liquid to create a paste. Slowly and firmly work in more flour, lifting it up with your hands as you work to create aeration. Add extra water a little at a time as required to gradually create a ball of sticky dough. Knead the ball of dough in the bowl for a few minutes to help it firm up.

Dust a clean work surface generously with flour and place the ball of dough on it. Knead the dough very firmly for several minutes, working it constantly until the surface is very smooth and almost shining, like grey stone. Wrap in clingfilm and set aside to rest for 30 minutes. (You will probably need a break yourself.)

Dust a large baking tray with flour and set aside ready to hold the cut noodles. Dust the work surface with more flour to prevent sticking. Using a very long rolling pin, roll out the dough to give a large, thin and rather square-ish circle. As you roll, turn the dough a quarter turn every so often and dust top and bottom with additional flour frequently. It will always seem too dry.

Fold the dough circle in half and dust with more flour, then fold again to give quarters and dust some more.

Use a large knife, and a thick, heavy ruler if you have one. Starting with the straight folded edges, cut firmly down through the layers of dough to give very fine noodles no more than 3mm/⅛in wide. Carefully transfer the noodles, which will be fragile, to the tray and sprinkle them with flour to prevent sticking.

To cook the noodles, bring a large pot of salted water to the boil. Add the noodles and cook for 20–60 seconds only, until tender but retaining some bite. Drain well, reserving the cooking liquid, and serve the noodles as desired. In Japan, the cooking liquid is taken to the table in a pot and served in cups to drink afterwards, flavoured to personal taste with a soy-based dipping sauce and spring onions.

RYE GNOCCHI WITH SPRING VEGETABLES

This is a classic gnocchi recipe in which the wheat flour is simply replaced with dark rich, sweet-tasting rye. I think white wheat flour is best for kneading the sticky dough, so this recipe is neither wheat nor gluten free. It's here because it's delicious and interesting.

SERVES 4

For the gnocchi
625g/1¼lb even-sized large potatoes
2 egg yolks
150g/5oz finely milled rye flour
Tipo 00 flour, or other strong white
    wheat flour, for dusting
salt and pepper

For the accompaniments
250g/8oz asparagus
150g/5oz fine green beans
150g/5oz Tenderstem or purple sprouting
    broccoli
a little olive oil, for frying
250g/8oz thick bacon rashers, chopped
50g/2oz baby spinach leaves
juice of 1 lemon
Parmesan cheese, to serve

COOK'S NOTES

❋ You could add some halved cherry tomatoes, peeled broad beans, basil leaves or ribbons of spring greens. Hispi cabbage is the logical choice for colder months, when the Parmesan could be replaced with fontina or Gorgonzola.

❋ Triticale is great here for its slightly milder flavour, but as with the rye, finely milled flour gives the best texture. If the consistency is mealy, your gnocchi will be woolly rather than silky. Similarly, it's important to rice the potatoes or put them through a mouli-legumes, because they need to be light and smooth. Lumpy mash equals lumpy gnocchi!

Boil the potatoes in their skins until they are tender when tested with a skewer and then drain. As soon as they are cool enough to handle, peel off the skins. Press them through a ricer into a large bowl. Add the egg yolks and season with salt and pepper. Gradually work in the rye flour to give a smooth, sticky dough.

Dust a work surface with Tipo 00 flour and flour a tray to hold your cut gnocchi. Take a portion of the dough and roll it into a long thin sausage 1.5cm/¾in in diameter. Cut the sausage into 1.5cm/¾in pillows and place them in a single layer on the flour-dusted tray. Cover with a tea towel while you continue to roll and cut batches of the remaining dough. The gnocchi can be sprinkled with a little more flour and kept under the tea towel for 1–2 hours before cooking, but they are best freshly made.

Bring a large saucepan of salted water to the boil and start on your accompaniments. Cut the asparagus, beans and broccoli into fork-able pieces and blanch them separately in the boiling water for 1–2 minutes, depending on thickness. Scoop them out and refresh under cold running water.

Add the gnocchi in batches to the boiling water. After 1–2 minutes they will rise to the surface of the water – once there, let them bubble at the top for a further minute before scooping them out into a wide colander.

Heat 1–2 tbsp olive oil in a skillet or other wide pan. Add the bacon and fry until browned and crisp. Remove the bacon and add the gnocchi to the pan in a single layer. Fry the pillows on each side until they are toasty brown, then return the bacon to the pan and toss. Add the spinach leaves, blanched vegetables and lemon juice, and toss until well combined, adding a little more olive oil if necessary.

Season to taste with salt and pepper and serve topped with shaved or grated Parmesan.

SPICY PRAWN AND QUINOA CAKES

Using really plump raw prawns and chopping them by hand makes a terrific difference to the luxurious succulence of these muffinish, kofta-esque cakes. I like to keep a bag of high-quality peeled raw prawns in the freezer for weeknight use and often buy online from the Fish Society. It's extremely convenient as long as you are aware of the protective ice glaze and whether you are measuring the defrosted weight or the gross frozen weight. If you are using unpeeled prawns, start with 275–300g/9–10oz as the wastage is typically 55 per cent.

MAKES 8

100g/3½oz quinoa
240ml/8fl oz fish, chicken or vegetable stock
125g/4oz raw green king prawn meat
2 spring onions, finely chopped
6 tbsp chopped coriander leaves
finely grated zest of 1 lime
2 tsp Sriracha hot chilli sauce, plus extra
   to serve
2 eggs
salt and pepper
oil, for greasing

Rinse the quinoa thoroughly in a very fine mesh sieve under cold water. Put it into a small saucepan and add the stock. Bring to the boil, then reduce the heat to low, cover and simmer for 8 minutes. Turn the heat off under the pan and leave the quinoa to steam for a further 10 minutes. Tip the cooked grain into a mixing bowl and leave to cool.

Using a large sharp knife, finely mince the prawn meat by hand (it will become too pasty if you use a processor) and add to the bowl of cooled quinoa. Add the spring onions along with the coriander, lime zest and Sriracha chilli sauce. Beat the eggs in a jug with plenty of salt and pepper, then pour into the bowl and stir to make a thick batter.

Heat the oven to 180°C/350°F/Gas 4 and grease 8 holes of a heavy cupcake tray with oil. Spoon the batter evenly into the holes and bake for 20–25 minutes, turning the tray halfway through cooking. The cakes are ready when the tops and edges are browned and the cakes have come away from the sides of the cupcake holes.

Remove from the oven and leave the cakes to stand in the tray for 5–10 minutes before removing with the help of a round-bladed knife and asbestos fingers. Serve with the extra chilli sauce.

COOK'S NOTES

✣ You could serve the cakes for lunch with salad and a dressing based on soy sauce or nam pla, or a creamy coriander and mint affair. I'm more inclined to just eat them plain, as they are a healthy and satisfying snack. The idea of making smaller ones to hand round at cocktail parties also appeals.

✣ Replace the king prawns with crabmeat if desired. (I utterly adore crab, but I think the prawn version better.)

✣ The bacon and cheese version is good too: leave out the prawns and lime zest. Instead add 125g/4oz each chopped bacon rashers and grated cheddar, and swap the coriander for parsley or rocket. Sriracha is fine here, but you could use any other thick red chilli sauce you have to hand – something with chipotle, for example.

GRAIN BURGERS

As much as I abhor imitation meat products, especially those produced by large factories, a decent grain burger recipe is a handy thing to have. The rules of making a good grain burger are extraordinarily similar to those for making good burgers from minced meat. A popular misconception is that homemade burgers require the addition of half the fridge's vegetable drawer, but in reality you only need a little seasoning. Even herbs are optional. Other flavours and textures belong in the bun along with the burger, not in the burger itself.

MAKES 4–6

300ml/½ pint vegetable stock
100g/3½oz freekeh
50g/2oz millet
50g/2oz brown rice
50g/2oz coarse or medium oatmeal
1 small garlic clove, crushed (optional)
4 tbsp chopped mixed herbs such as
    parsley, thyme, sage and chives
4 tsp soy sauce
a little olive or vegetable oil, for frying
salt and pepper

To serve (optional)
hamburger buns
green salad
relishes

Place the stock in a large saucepan with the freekeh, millet, brown rice and oatmeal, plus the garlic, if using. Bring the mixture to the boil and cook, stirring often, for 35–45 minutes or until all the water has been absorbed and the grains are breaking down.

Remove from the heat and stir in the herbs, soy sauce and salt and pepper to taste. Leave until cool enough to handle, then shape the mixture into burgers of the desired size, pressing them firmly together.

Heat a little oil in a heavy frying pan over a moderate heat and cook the burgers for 2–3 minutes on each side until browned. Serve in toasted hamburger buns with salad and relishes if desired.

COOK'S NOTES

❖ It's a basic rule but many get it wrong: if you put raw onion in the mixture, the burger will taste like raw onion. Burgers, whether meat or grain, cook more quickly than onion does. Why do you want an oniony taste anyway? If you do, there will be plenty in whatever chutney or relish you spread on the bun.

❖ Do not add grated carrot. It will not make the mixture taste better; it will help it fall apart.

❖ Beans and lentils are good additions to grain burgers but when used exclusively are often too soft and pasty, especially if the mistake is made of puréeing them in a food processor. If left firm, they tend to break up on frying. Cook them along with the grains so that they break down naturally.

❖ Its meaty flavour may make buckwheat seem like an ideal choice for grain burgers, but unless you adore buckwheat (and even if you do), it can taste too aggressive. Smoky-tasting freekeh, whole or cracked, is far better.

❖ The soluble fibre in the oatmeal makes this mixture adequately sticky. If you were to omit the oatmeal, you should consider adding a little beaten egg, but not a whole one. An alternative is to use another gluey grain, such as amaranth or teff.

❖ I was astonished on my first visit to San Francisco to find that it is the norm to serve alfalfa sprouts in burgers. Mind you, others would find the Australian insistence on beetroot very strange. In fact, both work well. So does a fried egg.

SWEETCORN FRITTERS

Sweetcorn fritters may seem complicated but in fact are very similar to pancakes. You don't even need to use a deep-fryer. They're also good fun for kids, who tend to enjoy picking out the little bits of corn embedded in the batter. Standard advice for cutting corn from the cob is to hold the cob vertically on a chopping board and cut down the sides with a large cook's knife. I find it less unwieldy to lie the corn on the board horizontally and use a small knife. The right way is the one that makes you feel most comfortable and safe.

MAKES 4–6

1 sweetcorn cob, husk and strings removed

75g/3oz plain wheat-type flour

2 tsp granulated sugar

½ tsp baking powder

¼ tsp cayenne pepper or paprika

a large pinch of salt

1 egg

4 tbsp milk

50g/2oz Cheddar cheese, finely diced

4 tbsp finely sliced spring onions

2 tbsp chopped coriander or parsley

2 tsp finely chopped chilli

a little olive or vegetable oil, for frying

pepper

Using a kitchen knife, cut the kernels from the sweetcorn cob. Scrape the cob with the back of the knife to squeeze out as much of the kernels and 'milk' as possible. Set aside.

Combine the flour, sugar, baking powder, cayenne or paprika and salt in a mixing bowl and make a well in the centre. In a small jug, whisk together the egg and milk and pour into the dry ingredients, stirring to make a very thick batter. Mix in the sweetcorn, cheese, spring onions, coriander or parsley, chilli and some freshly ground black pepper.

Heat a little oil in a large, heavy frying pan. Working on 2 or 3 fritters at a time, add large spoonfuls of the mixture to the pan and fry until the top is set and the bottom is golden. Flip over to brown on the other side, then remove from the pan and set aside in a warm place while you cook the remaining mixture. Serve hot, warm or cold.

COOK'S NOTES

✳ The added ingredients to the basic batter can be swapped with extreme ease. You only need to ensure you add around 4 tbsp of whatever chopped ingredients you desire. Parsnip and chorizo is an astonishingly good combo. Ham works well, so does chopped red bell pepper. You could also use finely chopped broccoli stems, or include cooked wild rice as one of the flavourings, but not in place of the sweetcorn.

✳ Serve as part of a brunch dish with spinach salad, grilled bacon and raw or roasted tomatoes. Alternatively, you could serve with a ready-made dipping sauce, relish or chutney chosen to suit the ingredients you have added to the batter.

✳ The mixture can be cooked into tiny pancakes to serve as canapés with smoked hams and fish, or guacamole and salsa.

JAPANESE SOBA PORRIDGE

Something of an acquired taste, this one, but an interesting use of buckwheat nevertheless. Try to find the milder-tasting whitish flour favoured by Japanese connoisseurs rather than the speckled, greyish flour commonly sold in Italian delicatessens and health food stores. The condiments are more than garnishes here. Their strong flavours are necessary to stand up to the powerful taste of the porridge. This recipe was given to me by London-based Japanese food writer Emi Kazuko. You may feel it serves two rather than one, at least the first time.

PER PERSON

½ tsp buckwheat kernels
½ tsp white sesame seeds
5 tbsp buckwheat flour
175ml/6fl oz water
a dab of wasabi paste

For the sauce
6 tbsp dashi (see page 162) or fish stock
4 tsp shoyu or dark soy sauce
4 tsp mirin
1½ tsp sugar

In a small saucepan, toast the buckwheat kernels for 3–5 minutes, stirring constantly, until browned and fragrant. Remove to a small bowl to cool. Repeat with the sesame seeds, add them to the buckwheat kernels and set aside.

Place the buckwheat flour and water in the same saucepan, stirring with a wooden spoon to give a smooth paste. Set the pan over a medium heat and cook, stirring constantly, until the porridge is soft and thick.

Transfer the mixture to a serving bowl and shape it into a mound. Top with a dab of wasabi paste, then sprinkle with the toasted seeds and set the bowl aside in a warm place.

Quickly clean out the saucepan and return it to the heat with all the sauce ingredients. Bring to the boil, stirring so that the sugar dissolves. Pour the sauce around the porridge and serve hot.

COOK'S NOTES

❖ I prefer to add a little chopped spring onion to the sauce for extra flavour. Some Japanese pickles served alongside would also be welcome, as their refreshing tang and crispness are a good contrast to the earthy flavour and smooth texture of the porridge.

❖ Instead of toasting the buckwheat and sesame seeds you could use furikake, the delicious ready-made Japanese seasoning blend of sesame seeds, shiso leaves and nori seaweed.

❖ Before you reject outright the idea of making your own wasabi paste from pure powdered wasabi and water, take a look at the list of additives on the tubes of ready-made wasabi paste now widely available. Now really, how hard is it to stir together a little powder and water?

HARD POLENTA

Some people dismiss polenta or mamaliga, as bland mush, but truly creative, talented cooks embrace it, seeing it as limited only by their own ideas. There is a lot of unnecessary Italian lore surrounding its making, but a heavy pan and long-handled spoon are musts. I find I have to add more water than other writers recommend, to keep it stirrable for the required cooking time. In South Africa they make krummelpap in this basic fashion but cover the pan so that the cornmeal steams, to give a crumbly texture.

SERVES 6–8

270g/15oz coarse cornmeal
a large pinch of salt
1 litre/1¾ pints water
a little oil for greasing

Place the cornmeal and salt in a large, heavy based saucepan. Slowly whisk in the water a little at a time and bring the mixture to the boil, stirring constantly.

Reduce the heat right down and simmer gently, stirring very frequently with a long-handled wooden spoon (it will spit fiercely), for 35–40 minutes or until the grains of starch have exploded and the mixture is very stiff and smooth and comes away from the sides of the pan when stirred. Alternatively, transfer the mixture to an oven heated to 180°C/350°F/Gas 4 and bake for 40 minutes, ensuring you use an ovenproof pan.

Tip the polenta out onto a lightly oiled wooden board or a warmed serving plate and shape into a mound. Cut into wedges for serving alongside Gorgonzola cheese, roast rabbit or fried fish.

COOK'S NOTES

❊ If you want to boost the taste of the polenta with cheese, mix in 200g/7oz grated Parmesan (or half-Parmesan and half-fontina) plus 100g/3½oz butter. Or add chopped herbs and olives to taste.

❊ A Swiss treatment of polenta is to serve the freshly cooked stiff mixture in a mound as an accompaniment to homemade beans in tomato sauce and thick slices of poaching sausage. Cotechino or bratwurst would be good used this way.

❊ Alternatively, grease a loaf tin or baking sheet with oil and, when the polenta is ready, pour it into the tin or onto the baking sheet and smooth over the surface. Leave to cool, then slice into squares or triangles, brush lightly with olive oil and grill until a golden crust forms. Serve with grilled or roast meats and stews.

❊ You can make chips by cutting the cooled polenta into sticks and frying in olive oil that has been flavoured with a few sliced garlic cloves and a sprig of rosemary. Drain thoroughly when cooked and salt generously before serving. If the browned garlic and rosemary finds its way into your mouth, so much the better.

❊ For lower-fat chips, spray with oil or Frylight and bake for 20–25 minutes at 180°C/350°F/Gas 4.

❊ Cut the set polenta into thick batons and wrap a wafer-thin slice of pancetta around the centre. Brush lightly with oil and roast at 180°C/350°F/Gas 4 for 20 minutes until the pancetta is cooked. These are ideal when served with drinks. You can always omit the pancetta and place a small cube of Gorgonzola cheese on the batons for the last 5 minutes that they are in the oven.

SOFT, CREAMY POLENTA

Italian food experts of my acquaintance would insist that this is not polenta but a cream of maize. My choice of cheese would be the distinctively square-shaped Taleggio, because I adore its fruity, herby, rather vegetal flavour, especially when just stirred into the hot cornmeal so that the creamy paste only slightly melts and the rind stays a little crusty. Like most rind-washed or smear-ripened cheeses, Taleggio's taste is milder than its aroma. The cheese originated in the Alpine region of northern Italy; its production has since spread but is nevertheless restricted by law.

SERVES 4–6

180g/6oz coarse cornmeal

1 tsp salt

1 litre/1¾ pints water

150–200g/5–7oz semi-soft Italian cheese, cubed

50g/2oz butter, cubed

pepper

Place the cornmeal and salt in a large, heavy saucepan. Slowly whisk in the water and bring the mixture to the boil, stirring constantly. Reduce the heat right down and simmer gently, stirring often, for 35 minutes. Alternatively, transfer the mixture to an oven heated to 180°C/350°F/ Gas 4 and bake for 40 minutes, ensuring you use an ovenproof pan.

Remove the pan from the heat and beat in the butter. Stir in the cubed cheese and season to taste with salt and freshly ground black pepper. Serve hot.

COOK'S NOTES

✳ Try polenta taragna, a mixture of buckwheat and corn, instead of plain cornmeal. The Moretti brand is good, but you can make your own version by combining 100g/3½oz buckwheat flour (a dark, coarse grind is preferable) with 200g/7oz of cornmeal.

✳ Other good additions to creamy polenta are chopped olives, sun-dried tomatoes, ham, piquant cured sausages and robust Mediterranean herbs, such as oregano and sage. Mix and match them, using Parmesan or pecorino cheese and/or olive oil as desired, to suit your own preferences. Remember to add plenty of black pepper.

✳ Walnuts and blue cheese is a particularly good combination in a dish such as this.

✳ The secret of the most delectable soft polenta often is, unfortunately, nothing more than beating in a very large pack of butter at the end of cooking. Skip the cheese on these occasions because you don't want to run the risk of adding anything remotely healthy like protein to this mixture. Top your buttery polenta with some fresh porcini, sliced and sautéed, with a little garlic, in lots of butter. It's a chilly weather dish, so you can wear big baggy jumpers for a week or two afterwards without looking too foolish.

✳ You can use any of these ideas with grits for a modern spin on Southwestern USA fare. Korean-American Edward Lee avoids cheese and instead cooks grits in chicken stock, stirring cold butter and soy sauce in just before serving.

✳ I like to cook polenta in a Crock-Pot too. It needs 1–2 hours on High, or 3–4 hours on Low. One of the company's own recipes, featuring chopped red bell pepper, paprika, cayenne and cumin (you can find it on the internet), is quite a favourite in our home.

LAYERED CORNMEAL WITH SPICY TOMATO SAUCE

This superb recipe was given to me by South Africa's highly esteemed restaurateur and food writer Peter Veldsman. Known locally as pap tart, it is a fascinating alternative to Italian recipes for layered and baked polenta, being very similar and yet noticeably different in its use of cinnamon, cumin and cayenne. My husband and I gorged ourselves on it the first time we made it, as it is so delicious. It features in Peter's excellent book *Flavours of South Africa*.

SERVES 6–8, IN THEORY

350g/11½oz coarse cornmeal

2 tsp salt

1 tsp cumin seeds

½ tsp cayenne pepper

1 litre/1¾ pints water

25g/1oz butter

100g/3½oz fontina or Parmesan cheese, sliced

For the sauce

2 tbsp olive or vegetable oil

2 large onions, sliced

1 cinnamon stick

1 tsp cumin seeds

3 garlic cloves, crushed

225ml/7½fl oz water

1.2kg/2½lb canned chopped tomatoes in juice

225ml/7½fl oz red wine

cayenne pepper, to taste

a large handful of basil leaves, torn

2 tsp chopped oregano or thyme

salt and pepper

Place the cornmeal, salt, cumin and cayenne in a large, heavy saucepan. Slowly whisk in the water and bring the mixture to the boil, stirring constantly. Lower the heat and simmer gently, stirring often, for 30 minutes. Stir in the butter, remove the pan from the heat and set aside.

Meanwhile, to make the sauce, heat the oil in a large saucepan and fry the onions, cinnamon and cumin until the onions are soft and translucent. Stir in the garlic, 2 tsp salt, pepper, to taste and the water, then bring to the boil. Add the tomatoes and wine, and simmer for 30–40 minutes until the mixture is very thick, stirring occasionally. Season to taste, adding the cayenne and fresh herbs. Discard the cinnamon.

Line a 20cm/8in square baking tin with foil so that it hangs over the rim. Press a layer of polenta into the base of the tin, smoothing over the surface. Cover with a layer of tomato sauce, then repeat the layers to fill the tin, ending with polenta. Chill, covered, for 1 hour to set.

Heat the oven to 160°C/325°F/Gas 3. Lay the sliced cheese over the top of the tart and bake for 20–25 minutes or until piping hot. Serve with your choice of accompaniments as desired (see Cook's Notes).

COOK'S NOTES

❖ Peter recommends serving the finished dish scattered with chopped chillies, fried garlic cloves and fresh coriander or basil leaves. Fried slices of aubergine and grilled or barbecued meats also make good accompaniments.

❖ Using red wine really lifts the tomato sauce, which is known as sheba in South Africa. You might want to include some chopped lavender in it too – another idea of Peter's.

SWEETCORN RISOTTO

Mixed grain risottos are proving a fun area of experimentation for many chefs. Here, the sweetcorn adds a pleasing fresh chewiness. Retaining the white rice is key when coaxing anyone wary of unusual grains into trying such a dish.

SERVES 4

850ml/1½ pints rich vegetable or chicken stock

2 large sweetcorn cobs, about 16cm/6½in long, husks and strings removed

6 spring onions

50g/2oz butter

1 tbsp olive oil

300g/10oz risotto rice

150ml/¼ pint white wine

50–75g/2–3oz Parmesan cheese, grated, plus extra to serve

salt and pepper

Put the stock into a small saucepan and bring slowly to the boil. Meanwhile, remove the kernels from the sweetcorn and place them in a bowl with the creamy juices they exude. Break up any clusters of kernels, then set aside. Chop the spring onions, keeping the white and green parts separate.

In a large, heavy saucepan, melt half the butter with the oil over a moderate heat. Add the white parts of the spring onions and sauté for 5 minutes or until soft and tender but not browned.

Add the rice and cook for a few minutes, stirring, until the grains are shiny and becoming translucent. Pour in the wine and keep stirring the rice until the liquid bubbles away.

Add a ladle of the simmering stock and make a note of the time. Cook, stirring constantly, until the rice has absorbed all the stock. Then add another ladle of hot stock and repeat the process.

Once you have been adding stock and stirring the risotto for 15 minutes, add the corn kernels, their juices and 4 heaped tbsp of the reserved green parts of the spring onions. Continue adding stock and stirring the risotto for 5 minutes.

Turn off the heat and stir in the cheese and the remaining butter. Season to taste with salt and pepper. Sprinkle with a little of the leftover spring onions and serve immediately with extra Parmesan.

COOK'S NOTES

❖ Substitute any well-flavoured grating cheese such as Cheddar, pecorino, Manchego or, given the American inspiration of this recipe, Dry Monterey Jack.

❖ If you want to add herbs, think basil, coriander or parsley. A little red or green chilli works here, too.

❖ The stripped corn cobs can be used to make corn stock (see page 51). Using corn stock in this dish gives a paler and more delicately flavoured result than rich vegetable or chicken stock do.

❖ The sky will not fall in if you make up some powdered vegetable bouillon using fresh boiling water and add it from a jug at the side of the stove rather than from a simmering pan. Note that most chefs have also risked hell-fire and damnation by not stirring risotto constantly for 20 minutes.

❖ Add protein in the form of crisp-cooked bacon over the top, grilled prawns (see page 160), marinated beef kebabs or some slices of barbecued, grilled or roasted chicken (see pages 160–1) or turkey.

CRAB WITH BUCKWHEAT AND SPELT

How you approach this recipe depends on how you buy your crab. I'm all for meticulously making the shellfish stock and flavoured butter if you have good raw materials to work with, but on other occasions I'm very happy with a few dumbed-down alternatives that turn this from a dinner party dish into an easy midweek supper.

SERVES 4

250g/8oz pearled spelt

125g/4oz buckwheat

2 tbsp olive oil

2 large banana shallots, finely chopped

200ml/7fl oz dry white wine or Noilly Prat vermouth

300ml/½ pint shellfish stock (see page 160)

275–325g/9–11oz white crabmeat

50g/2oz rocket leaves or baby spinach

2–3 tbsp finely chopped chives

2–3 tbsp finely chopped tarragon

½ tsp finely chopped pickled chillies

25g/1oz shellfish butter (see page 160)

salt and pepper

If you are making the shellfish stock and butter yourself, prepare these first.

Cook the spelt and buckwheat separately in a generous quantity of boiling salted water until almost tender: the spelt should take about 15 minutes and the buckwheat 8 minutes. Drain and refresh under cold running water, then set aside to drain thoroughly.

Heat the oil in a wide pan and fry the shallots until soft. Add the spelt and buckwheat to the pan and cook, stirring, for a couple of minutes, then add the wine or vermouth and simmer until the liquid seems to have evaporated. Pour in the stock (for this method there's no particular reason to heat it first) and cook, stirring, over a medium-high heat until the grains are al dente.

Stir in the crabmeat, rocket or spinach, chives, tarragon and chillies, then add the shellfish butter. Taste and adjust the seasonings as desired before serving.

COOK'S NOTES

❖ A few convenience products I really like are the Fish Society's frozen packs and batons of white crabmeat, as well as Costco's Chicken of the Sea longlife tubs, which are a different level of quality, but still extremely enjoyable. German company Jürgen Langbein produces a decent shellfish stock cube.

❖ I'm very keen on keeping homemade flavoured butters in the freezer – they offer a lot of reward for very little effort. Shellfish butters are more labour intensive than herb and spice ones; the easiest method is to use prawn shells rather than crab shells, as they are soft enough to put in a small food processor.

❖ The point here is to mix the spelt and buckwheat with crab, but you could certainly do this dish with one or the other, or replace the spelt with pearled barley or rice.

❖ My husband favours a version of this dish with a heaped tablespoon of French mustard instead of the chillies. Martin Benn of Sydney's Sepia restaurant serves a crab and buckwheat risotto (the recipe for it is readily available online) that includes both Dijon and wholegrain mustards among several other ingredients (and yes, shellfish foam) befitting a high-end restaurant.

❖ If by chance (ha!) you have a few spoonfuls of bisque lying around, warm it through and drizzle over the finished dish as a garnishing sauce.

BARLEY 'RISOTTO'

Pearl barley risotto (or orzotto – *orzo* is the Italian word for barley) has become the tired chef's go-to when they need to stick something vegetarian on a menu. Soon it will be as ubiquitous as vegetable lasagne seemed in the 1990s – pity. Australian celebrity chef Luke Mangan has a more creative way with it: surrounding the grains with coconut broth and topping with roast barramundi. When I asked him why he thought the unusual combination would work, he confessed that some free-flowing alcohol while jetting to America may have been a factor in its inception.

SERVES 4

1.25 litres/4fl oz fish or chicken stock

25g/1oz butter

1 tbsp olive or vegetable oil

2 shallots, finely chopped

200g/7oz pearled or semi-pearled barley

150ml/¼ pint white wine

4 tbsp cream or coconut cream, or to taste

a handful of chopped flat-leaf parsley

salt and pepper

Put the stock into a saucepan and bring slowly to the boil. Meanwhile, in a large, heavy saucepan, melt the butter with the oil over a moderate heat. Add the shallots and sauté for 5 minutes or until soft.

Add the barley and cook for 3 minutes, stirring, until the grains are shiny. Pour in the wine and stir until it bubbles away. Add a ladle of hot stock. Cook, stirring constantly, until the barley has absorbed all the stock. Then add another ladle of hot stock and repeat the process. Continue until the barley is tender, adding hot water as necessary once all the stock has been incorporated.

Stir in the cream or coconut cream and the parsley. Season to taste and serve.

COOK'S NOTES

❋ First know your barley. White, polished pearl barley is normally favoured for this type of dish because it releases its starch readily, yet it can be difficult to buy. The slightly beige semi-pearled barley is nuttier, chewier and requires longer cooking but is still very pleasant, if not better.

❋ If you are using semi-pearled barley, start adding hot water after this measure of stock has been incorporated, otherwise the dish will taste too strongly of reduced stock.

❋ An alternative method of cooking barley is to boil semi-pearled or pot barley in water for about 30 minutes, then drain and cook as for traditional risotto. Or you could simply cook the barley until tender in stock, drain and sauté with some cream or mascarpone and chopped herbs.

❋ This last technique is used by French chef Emmanuel Leblay for making a 'risotto' of petit épeautre, featured in Patricia Wells' *The Paris Cookbook*. Semi-pearled farro can also be used in this fashion. Served with roast chicken and a sauce of warmed reduced chicken stock, it is superb, and remarkably easy.

❋ For pan-roast fish and coconut broth recipes, see pages 161 and 163 respectively.

GENMAI GOMOKU

The West increasingly appreciates that Japanese do a lot more with rice than make sushi. Gomoku meshi, in which a variety of tasty morsels are simmered with rice in a pot, is a good example. The Japanese don't, however, as a rule appreciate brown rice, which this version features. It is an excellent way to use all those delicious plump, short-grained brown rices that can be found in fashionable organic stores. Women will be particularly gratified to find such a moreish way of consuming those intriguing packs of snow-dried tofu and seaweed too.

SERVES 4

4 squares snow-dried tofu

5g/¼oz hijiki seaweed

400g/13oz short-grain brown rice

850ml/1½ pints dashi (see page 162), fish or
　　vegetable stock

4 tbsp soy sauce

2 tbsp mirin

4 fresh shiitake mushrooms, stems discarded
　　and sliced

1 small carrot, sliced

1 small turnip or mooli (daikon), diced

Place the tofu in a small heatproof bowl. Cover with warm water and leave to soak for 5 minutes. Squeeze the tofu to release the milky liquid, then discard the water and soak again. Repeat the process 4–5 times or until the water that oozes from the tofu is no longer milky. Meanwhile, soak the hijiki according to the packet instructions.

Rinse the rice, drain and place in a large pot or casserole. Add the stock, soy sauce and mirin, cover and bring to the boil. Reduce the heat and simmer for 25 minutes.

Using scissors, cut the squares of drained tofu into quarters. Cut any large pieces of hijiki. When the rice has been cooking for 25 minutes, lift the lid and scatter in the tofu, seaweed, mushrooms, carrot and turnip or mooli. Cover again and continue cooking for 15 minutes until the liquid is absorbed and the ingredients are tender.

Turn off the heat and leave the pot to stand, covered, for 10 minutes. Lift the lid, stir the rice very gently and spoon into warm bowls to serve.

COOK'S NOTES

✣ If you would like to add some fresh greenery to this dish, add 12 trimmed mangetout or sugar snap peas to the pot a few minutes before the rice is scheduled to finish cooking.

✣ Dried shiitake can be used instead of fresh, in which case the flavoured soaking water can be strained and used in place of some of the stock. Remember to discard the tough stems.

✣ This is a good opportunity to practise your carrot carving skills; it really enhances the look of the dish. To do this, cut 4 or 5 equidistant little grooves down the length of the peeled carrot before slicing it.

CHICKEN WITH FREEKEH

Allspice, also known as Jamaica pepper, makes a terrific seasoning, especially for chicken. The name refers to the taste, which is reminiscent of a blend of spices such as nutmeg and cloves. Do not confuse it with products such as five-spice powder, which really are a blend of spices. Although native to the tropical areas of the Americas, it is a distinguishing characteristic of Arabian cooking. This recipe is based on one from Lebanese food expert Anissa Helou.

SERVES 6-8

1 medium whole chicken
300g/10oz freekeh
2 litres/3½ pints water
3 cinnamon sticks
½ tsp allspice berries
85g/3¼oz butter (optional)
¼ tsp pepper
a handful each of parsley, coriander and
    mint, roughly chopped
lemons, halved, to serve
salt

Rinse the chicken and place it in a heavy stockpot with the freekeh, water and cinnamon. Bring to the boil and skim any froth that develops on the surface of the water. Cover the pot and reduce the heat to medium-low. Cook the chicken for 1 hour, being sure not to let the water boil hard.

Meanwhile, toast the allspice berries in a dry frying pan until fragrant, stirring constantly. Transfer to a mortar and crush until fine.

When the chicken is done, use 2 large forks to lift it carefully from the cooking liquid. Make sure you tilt the cavity of the chicken downwards so that the hot liquid secreted inside runs back into the pot.

Place the chicken on a large baking tray and set aside to cool slightly. Remove the cinnamon sticks from the pot and discard, then turn the heat under the pot to low. Cover the pot and leave the freekeh to continue cooking gently while you remove and discard the skin from the bird. Shred the flesh from the bones and then into bite-sized pieces. Stir the chicken meat into the freekeh and continue cooking for 20 minutes, adding more water if the pan becomes too dry.

Meanwhile, if desired, melt the butter in a saucepan and cook until it is nut-brown. Stir the butter into the freekeh stew. Season with the allspice and pepper, adding salt to taste. Scatter over the chopped herbs. Serve hot, with the lemon halves.

COOK'S NOTES

✣ This can also be made (and authentically so) with wheatberries or barley. In these cases, the cooked chicken is traditionally cut into small pieces and beaten into the grain mixture so that the dish is more like a savoury porridge.

✣ According to Anissa, a shoulder of lamb, trimmed of fat, can be used in place of chicken.

LOVELY LAMB STEW

Stew is not one of the English language's most enticing words and, as a result, many wonderful dishes are being ignored. Revisiting the old-fashioned British lamb stew was one of the great delights of compiling this book. The preparation is almost mindless and yet with long, slow cooking the ingredients meld into a creation that tastes as though it took a clever chef a lot of effort to produce. There is no need for side dishes. All that's required to make it look sumptuous is a variety of vegetables.

SERVES 4–6

100g/3½oz semi-pearled or pot barley
2 tbsp oil
950g/2lb lamb chops with bones,
    such as those from the neck end
2 small parsnips, cubed
1 medium onion, chopped
1 large leek, thickly sliced
250g/8oz carrots, cubed
250g/8oz swede, cubed
4 small potatoes, quartered
1 bouquet garni, made by tying together
    a small length of celery, a bay leaf, a few
    sprigs of thyme and some parsley stalks
water, stock, ale or cider, to cover
a handful of chopped parsley
salt and pepper

Put the barley in a saucepan, cover generously with water and bring to the boil. Reduce the heat and simmer for 15–20 minutes to part-cook it.

Meanwhile, in a large flameproof casserole, heat the oil. Working in batches, add the lamb and brown the meat on each side. Remove to a plate and add the parsnips, onion, leek, carrots and swede to the pot and cook, stirring occasionally, for 3 minutes until they begin to soften. Scoop any excess fat from the pan. Heat the oven to 180°C/350°F/Gas 4.

Drain the barley and add it to the pot with the browned meat, potatoes and bouquet garni. Season with some salt and pepper, then pour in just enough water, stock, ale or cider to come about 1cm/½in under the top of the ingredients in the pot. Cover and bring to the boil, then transfer the casserole to the oven to cook for 2 hours.

About 15 minutes before the end of cooking, stir the chopped parsley into the casserole. Remove the bouquet garni and season to taste before serving.

COOK'S NOTES

❊ Terrific though barley is, this dish also works well with short-grain brown rice and wheatberries.
❊ In his book *Appetite*, Nigel Slater suggests that stews such as this are especially good made with duck or guinea fowl as well as the more predictable chicken.
❊ If preferred, replace the root vegetables in this dish with canned tomatoes, a little celery, a bell pepper and some black or green olives. Add less liquid (you could use wine) to compensate for the juiciness of the tomatoes.

MUSHROOM RAGOUT WITH BARLEY

According to the *Larousse Gastronomique*, the French word *ragout* dates from 1642 and was once used to describe anything that stimulated the appetite. Today, ragout is understood to mean a stew made from meat, poultry, game, fish or vegetables cooked in a thickened flavoured liquid. However, ragouts of vegetables and mushrooms are usually cooked in their own juices after first browning the ingredients. This hearty recipe comes from Poland, where wild mushrooms are rather commonplace.

SERVES 4

15g/½oz dried morels
15g/½oz dried porcini
700ml/1¼ pints chicken or vegetable stock
25g/1oz butter
1 large onion, finely chopped
1 celery stick, finely diced
100g/3½oz semi-pearled or pot barley
1 bay leaf
½ tsp salt
300g/10oz mixed selection of fresh exotic and wild mushrooms, preferably including chanterelles
2 tbsp soured cream or crème fraîche
a handful of chopped parsley

Pick over and clean the dried morels and porcini as necessary. Place the stock in a large saucepan and bring to the boil. Turn off the heat and add the dried mushrooms. Set aside to infuse for 30 minutes.

Melt half the butter in a frying pan and add the chopped onion and celery. Sauté for 2 minutes, then lower the heat right down, cover and cook gently for about 20 minutes until soft and sweet, stirring occasionally.

Using a slotted spoon, scoop the soaked mushrooms out of the stock and squeeze the excess liquid back into the saucepan. Roughly chop the rehydrated mushrooms and return them to the stock.

Add the onion and celery to the stock with the barley, bay leaf and salt. Bring to the boil, cover and simmer over a very low heat for 45–50 minutes or until the barley is just tender and hardly any liquid remains in the saucepan. If the pan boils dry, top it up with a little hot water from the kettle.

Meanwhile, clean and trim the fresh mushrooms as necessary and, if large, cut into generous bite-sized pieces. Melt the remaining butter in a frying pan and sauté the fresh mushrooms for 5 minutes until just cooked.

When the barley is ready, stir the sautéed mushrooms into it, then the soured cream or crème fraîche. Serve sprinkled with chopped parsley.

COOK'S NOTES

- This looks better and is more enjoyable to eat if the cool cream is folded in just a little so that there are pockets of creaminess, rather than stirring until it is thoroughly combined. Alternatively, serve the fresh sautéed mushrooms on a bed of the barley stew and use the cream more like a sauce, drizzling some over the mushrooms and stirring some into the ragout.
- Wild rice, wholegrain rice and wheatberries are good alternatives to barley in this dish. A portion of rye could be mixed into the barley too.

SHELLFISH AND SAFFRON STEW

Rich saffron sauce, thickened with eggs and cream, is a sensuous complement to the fresh shellfish and spiky black wild rice used in this luxurious dish. It's a real dinner party special that is as delectable visually as it is on the palate, yet relatively simple. Saffron is often held up as an expensive ingredient, but it is tremendously good value, as a little goes a very long way.

SERVES 6–8

200g/7oz wild rice

½ tsp saffron threads

1 tbsp hot water

5 egg yolks

500ml/17fl oz cream

300ml/½ pint fish stock

300ml/½ pint dry white wine

750g/1½lb raw prawns, peeled and shells reserved, plus 6 extra, to serve

750g/1½lb shelled scallops

5 mussels in their shells, scrubbed

2 tbsp olive oil

4 tbsp parsley leaves, chopped (optional)

salt and pepper

COOK'S NOTES

❋ Any wholegrain rice works well in this dish, as does black barley. If you rinse coloured rices after cooking, they will not leach too much into the cream sauce. An advantage of wild rice, though, is that its colour does not bleed at all.

❋ I've had equal success making this with large pieces of firm white and pink fish in place of the scallops and prawns. In fact, the recipe would work terrifically well with poached chicken too.

❋ Include some vegetables if you like, especially sliced leeks and carrots, cooked briefly after you have removed the mussels from the pot.

Cook the wild rice in a large saucepan with a generous quantity of boiling salted water.

Meanwhile, in a dry pan, toast the saffron for 2 minutes or until crisp and fragrant. Transfer to a mortar and crush until fine. Add the hot water to dilute the saffron.

In a large mixing bowl, beat together the egg yolks and cream, then add the saffron liquid and set aside to infuse for 30 minutes.

Once cooked, drain and rinse the wild rice under cold running water and set aside. In a stockpot, combine the fish stock and wine and bring to the boil. Add the prawns and scallops and immediately remove from the heat. Allow to steep for 3 minutes, then use a slotted spoon to remove the shellfish from the stock.

Return the stock to simmering point. Add the mussels, cover the pot and cook until the mussels have opened, about 3–5 minutes. Remove them from the pan with a slotted spoon and set aside. Discard any that do not open.

Add the reserved prawn shells to the stockpot and bring it to the boil. Boil vigorously over a high heat for 20 minutes or until the stock has reduced to a volume of about 250ml/7¾fl oz and has intensified in flavour.

Line a sieve with a double thickness of muslin and pour the stock through it into a large jug or bowl. Discard the solids.

Slowly whisk the hot stock into the saffron cream, then return the mixture to the pot. Add the cooked wild rice, prawns and scallops and heat through over a low heat. As soon as it is hot, add the mussels, turn off the heat, cover the pot and leave to stand for 1 minute so that the mussels just warm through.

In a frying pan over a medium heat, fry the remaining prawns in the oil for 3 minutes on each side.

Season the mixture to taste with salt and freshly ground black pepper. Ladle the stew into bowls, garnish with the prawns and parsley, if desired, and serve.

GRÜNKOHL

Pat Lawrence, husband of my food writer friend Sue Lawrence, has the dubious distinction of having been twice crowned Grünkohl Konig of his local village while living in Ostfriesland. The award is not for cooking the stew but for eating vast quantities of it. Grünkohl dinners often take place after inter-village matches of bosseln, a rowdy winter sport involving on-street bowling and a great deal of schnaps. Pat remembers them being 'like an Ostfriesich Burns night, but without the speeches and poetry'.

SERVES 4

- 2 tbsp vegetable oil
- 2 onions, chopped
- 1.25kg/2½lb spring or collard greens
- 500g/1lb gammon or bacon joint, presoaked if necessary
- 500ml/17fl oz water
- 3 tbsp coarse oatmeal or oat groats
- 2–4 wurst or other fresh sausages
- salt and pepper

Heat the oil in a large, heavy flameproof casserole over a moderate heat. Add the onions, reduce the heat and cook gently for 10 minutes or until the onions are soft, stirring occasionally.

Meanwhile, trim the greens, separate the leaves from the stems and chop roughly. Add to the onions and cook, stirring frequently, for 5 minutes.

Lay the gammon or bacon joint in the casserole and pour in the water. Cover and cook over a very gentle heat, using a heat diffuser if necessary, for 1 hour, stirring occasionally to prevent sticking. Add more water if the pan becomes dry.

Add the oatmeal or groats, plus a little more water if necessary (this will depend on how gentle the heat is), then cover again and cook for 30 minutes, stirring occasionally. Lay the sausages in the casserole and continue cooking for another 30 minutes.

Season to taste with pepper and, if necessary, some salt, although the mixture should already be rather salty, thanks to the cured meat. Serve hot, with boiled potatoes, beer and schnaps if desired.

COOK'S NOTES

- The first time I made this, the pan boiled dry near the end of cooking and some of the greens turned rather brown. It was still really lovely.
- Oats are a revelation in this type of stew, their creamy texture and sweet taste balancing the saltiness of the meat and the bitterness of the greens. But you could certainly use barley, wheat, wholegrain rice or rye.
- A leafy Savoy or other green cabbage will work fine in place of spring or collard greens.
- If you can't find wurst, go for a mild herbed or spiced sausage. It doesn't really matter what type you choose. I have even used Toulouse sausages with great success in this recipe.

POSOLE VERDE

Authenticity of dishes is to be admired in food writing, but there's something about a recipe asking you to skin and bone a pig's head that doesn't inspire most people. That's why I use this posole recipe based on one from Dean & Deluca's cookbook, rather than one from the great authorities on Mexican cuisine. The meat can be bought ready-prepared from your butcher. The only thing stopping me calling it a quick and easy dish is the fact that the corn grains need lengthy soaking and cooking.

SERVES 6

175g/6oz red posole
175g/6oz green chillies
2 tbsp vegetable oil
1 large onion, finely sliced
2 garlic cloves, finely chopped
450g/14½oz boned pork shoulder, cubed
4 chicken thigh fillets, quartered
50g/2oz coriander, chopped
4 tbsp lime juice
salt and pepper

To serve
1 avocado, diced
1 small onion, finely chopped
a small bowl of tortilla chips

Soak the posole in a bowl of cold water for 3 hours or as directed on the packet.

Meanwhile, roast the chillies whole over a naked flame or under a very hot grill until the skins turn black and have blistered and charred. Place the chillies in a plastic bag to steam the skins loose. When cool enough to handle, peel and deseed them. Chop the flesh coarsely and set aside.

In a large, heavy pot or casserole, heat the vegetable oil. Add the sliced onion and cook over a moderate heat, stirring often, for 8 minutes or until the onion is soft. Add the garlic and cook for another 2 minutes.

Add the pork, chicken and the roasted chillies to the pot and cook, stirring frequently, for 10 minutes or until the meat has started to brown.

Drain the posole and add it to the pot. Pour in enough hot water to just cover the meat. Bring to the boil, then reduce the heat right down, half-cover the pot and cook the stew gently for 2 hours or until the posole is full-blown and the meat is meltingly tender. Add some more water if the liquid reduces too quickly.

Season to taste, then sprinkle with the chopped coriander and lime juice. Serve accompanied by separate bowls of diced avocado, chopped onion and tortilla chips.

COOK'S NOTES

✳ Hominy can be used in place of red posole, which I prefer for its stunning appearance, but it can be difficult to find.
✳ Don't skimp on the coriander and lime juice. Yes, it does seem like a huge quantity but they make the stew taste wonderfully fresh and aromatic.
✳ Almost any green chilli will do. People from the Americas may baulk at this idea, but in other countries we usually have to make do with what we can get and in this case the differences in flavour do not present a huge problem.

GRAIN-BASED STUFFINGS FOR CHICKEN

A good independent butcher is a terrific asset to the cook, not just for careful sourcing of the best meats and poultry but also for knife skills. They can perform the fussy prep work essential for spectacular food presentations for you (and are often keen to be asked to do so).

SERVES 6

1 chicken, about 1.9–2kg/3¾–4lb, boned
butter, for smearing

For the stuffing
200g/7oz wild rice
1 tbsp olive or vegetable oil
1 small onion, finely chopped
1 celery stick, finely chopped
4 tbsp Madeira
75g/3oz dried cranberries or cherries
50g/2oz roughly chopped pecans or walnuts
1 tsp parsley leaves, or ½ tsp thyme leaves, chopped
salt and pepper

COOK'S NOTES

✳ This basic recipe is easily varied. For a Middle Eastern flavour, replace the wild rice with freekeh, the dried cranberries with chopped dried apricots, the pecans with skinned almonds, pistachios or pine kernels (or a mixture) and the Madeira with white wine, and add some ground cinnamon and allspice to the simmering onion and celery. Bulgur wheat will also work beautifully with these flavourings.

✳ If you like Lyn Hall's quinoa salad (see page 67), replace the wild rice with quinoa (cooking it for only 12 minutes), the dried fruit with fresh grapes, the pecans with toasted cashews and the Madeira with white wine, and add some grated lime zest.

To make the stuffing, cook the wild rice in a saucepan of boiling salted water for 45–50 minutes. Meanwhile, in a frying pan, heat the oil and add the onion. Cook for 5 minutes, stirring often, then add the celery and continue cooking for 5 minutes until the onion is soft and golden. Add the Madeira and simmer, stirring occasionally, until it has evaporated. Leave to cool.

Drain and rinse the cooked wild rice thoroughly under cold running water, then drain again. Place it in a large bowl. Add the onion mixture, dried fruit, nuts, herbs and salt and pepper to taste.

Heat the oven to 220°C/425°F/Gas 7. Open out the boned chicken skin-side down on a work surface and pile the stuffing mixture into the centre, patting it together with your hands. Wrap the body back around the stuffing and use a large needle and kitchen string to sew the chicken back together, working from the neck end right down the back of the bird to the tail.

Pat the chicken into shape and rub generously all over with butter. Season with salt and pepper. Place the chicken breast-side down in a roasting tin and roast for 20 minutes. Then reduce the heat to 190°C/375°F/Gas 5 and cook a further 20 minutes.

Remove the tin from the oven and turn the chicken onto its back. Baste well and return to the oven for 25–40 minutes or until the juices run clear when the thickest part of the thigh is pierced with a skewer.

Transfer the chicken to a carving plate and leave to stand for 10–15 minutes. Meanwhile, drain the cooking juices from the tin into a jug and pour over the chicken when serving.

FREEKEH PILAF

Green wheat freekeh's distinctive smoky taste, as well as its high levels of usable protein and fibre, make it an ideal base for vegetarian main courses. Adding nuts and fruit in typical Middle Eastern style enhances the flavour and increases the nutritional punch that this intriguing grain packs. This delicious, luxurious recipe is derived from one in Sonia Uvezian's excellent *Recipes and Remembrances from an Eastern Mediterranean Kitchen,* in which she interestingly notes that freekeh is referred to in the Bible by the name 'parched corn'.

SERVES 4

60g/2¼oz pistachios
¼ tsp allspice berries
3 tbsp olive oil
1 onion, finely chopped
200g/7oz freekeh
570ml/18fl oz vegetable stock
15g/1 tbsp butter
50g/2oz dried apricots, sliced
6 tbsp raisins or sultanas
½ tsp ground cinnamon
salt and pepper

In a dry heavy frying pan, toast the pistachios over a medium to low heat, stirring constantly, until lightly browned and fragrant. Transfer to a bowl to cool. Repeat using the allspice berries, but transfer them once toasted to a mortar and crush finely.

In a large casserole, heat the olive oil. Add the onion and cook for 10 minutes or until soft and golden. Add the freekeh and cook, stirring, for 2 minutes. Pour in the stock and bring the mixture to a boil. Lower the heat, cover the pan and simmer for 30 minutes or until the liquid is absorbed and the grains are tender.

Meanwhile, in the frying pan, gently melt the butter. Add the apricots, raisins, crushed allspice and cinnamon and cook, stirring frequently, over a medium-low heat until the fruit is plump and just starting to turn golden.

Roughly chop the toasted pistachios and stir them into the cooked freekeh. Stir in the sautéed fruit and adjust the seasoning to taste with salt and pepper. Serve hot.

COOK'S NOTES

* Following this basic recipe you can also make pilafs based on bulgur wheat and rice. Reduce the quantity of liquid to 340ml/11½fl oz and cut the cooking time to 15 minutes.
* Slivered almonds or pine kernels may be used instead of pistachios, but the colour of pistachios enhances the presentation. Alternatively, use prunes or a little chopped preserved lemon instead of the dried apricots.
* Precede this dish with a selection of mezze based on fresh veg, such as green beans cooked in a sauce of tomato and onion, and a plate of crudités with herbs.
* This pilaf makes an excellent side dish for grilled chicken fillets (see page 160) seasoned with a little crushed allspice, or roast lamb (see page 161). You can also use it as a poultry stuffing by following the technique on page 103 using ready-boned chicken.

FARRO, PINE KERNEL AND SULTANA SAUTE

The scrumptious-sounding combination of wheat grains, pine kernels and sultanas goes back at least as far as Roman times. It features in *Apicius*, also known as *The Roman Cookery Book*, generally recognized as the first published collection of recipes. This sauté can be made and served without the chicken, but the flavour really benefits from being cooked in the same pan.

SERVES 2

1½ tbsp semi-pearled farro or other
    semi-pearled wheat-type grain
2 chicken breast fillets
2 tbsp olive oil
2 tbsp chicken or meat stock
4 tbsp pine kernels
4 tbsp sultanas
1 tbsp balsamic vinegar
salt and pepper
a handful of chopped parsley, to serve

Place the farro in a small saucepan with a generous quantity of salted water and bring to the boil. Reduce the heat and simmer for 25–35 minutes or until the farro is tender.

Meanwhile, place a chicken fillet under a sheet of clingfilm and use a mallet or heavy rolling pin to flatten it evenly. Repeat with the other fillet.

When the farro is done, rinse it thoroughly and drain well. Heat the olive oil in a very large frying pan. Add the chicken and cook for 2–3 minutes on each side until cooked through. Remove from the pan and set aside in a warm place.

Pour the stock into the frying pan and stir vigorously with a wooden spoon to dissolve the caramelized cooking juices from the chicken. Add the farro, pine kernels and sultanas and sauté for 5 minutes until the pine kernels start to brown and the sultanas are plump.

Add the vinegar to the pan and toss to combine. When the moisture in the pan has evaporated, season the grain mixture to taste with salt and pepper and serve with the sliced cooked chicken breasts, sprinkled with the parsley.

COOK'S NOTES

✻ Farro expands a lot on cooking, so unless you want leftovers, you raise the seemingly tiny quantity given here at your peril. There should be an equal volume of cooked grain (4 tbsp) to pine kernels and sultanas in the finished dish.

✻ Mix in a handful of chopped parsley towards the end of cooking if desired.

✻ One of chef Giorgio Locatelli's signature dishes is based on similar but more complex lines. He uses duck breasts, and they would certainly work here, but remember to spoon the vast quantities of fat they produce out of the pan before adding the grains and pine kernels.

✻ For a vegetarian dish, cook some baby Savoy cabbages while the farro is boiling. Heat the oil in the frying pan and simply sauté the grains, pine kernels and sultanas in that, then mix in the vinegar and season. Serve the sauté over the cooked, drained cabbage, which you have cut into wedges and arranged on a plate.

✻ Crab apple or sour grape verjus (or verjuice), another modern and yet ancient ingredient, can be used in place of the balsamic vinegar for a lighter but still strongly fruity taste.

HERRING IN OATMEAL

Herring is native to the North Atlantic but overlooked in the UK, despite it being rich in healthy fish oils. In his *New Delicatessen Food Handbook*, Glynn Christian theorizes that its lack of popularity in Britain may result from the fish's former association with poverty, but I suspect it's simply down to the bones. There's a lot of them, and for the inexperienced, eating your way round them takes a degree of practice and patience. Do not be concerned if you accidentally consume some; they are soft enough to eat and rich in calcium.

SERVES 2

50g/2oz medium or pinhead oatmeal
4 herrings, part-boned if desired
8 large rashers fatty bacon
a little vegetable oil or butter
a little mustard, to serve
salt and pepper

Spread the oatmeal on a plate and season it with salt and pepper. Press the fish into the oatmeal, turning them to coat evenly on both sides.

Place the bacon in a large, heavy frying pan and set over a low heat. Slowly cook so that the fat from the bacon melts a little into the pan to provide the cooking medium for the fish. Cook until the bacon is a little browned, then remove from the pan and keep warm.

Place the coated fish in the pan and add a little oil or butter if there doesn't seem to be enough fat to fry the fish. Cook over a moderate heat for 3 minutes on each side or until the fish is cooked through. Serve with the bacon and a little mustard.

COOK'S NOTES

* The oatmeal should stick easily to fresh fish. If they're a bit older, place them briefly under cold running water and shake dry before coating in the oatmeal.
* The idea behind this traditional method of cooking herring is that the fish will be flavoured by the bacon fat. If you would rather cook the fish in oil and butter, that's fine. If you prefer, you can use herring fillets instead of whole fish, or trout instead of herring.
* The method of simply pressing the fish into the oatmeal works equally well with cornmeal. In this case you can keep the seasoning to just salt and pepper, or add a mixture of herbs and spices. For a 'blackened' flavour, combine 2 tbsp cornmeal with 3 small crushed garlic cloves, plus 1 tsp each cayenne pepper, fennel seeds, dried oregano and thyme, and plenty of salt and pepper.
* Another good option is a 50:50 mixture of coconut flour and hemp flour with plenty of salt and pepper. The deep grassy taste of the hemp is nicely tempered and sweetened by the coconut.
* You can place the crumbing in a plastic bag, add the food to be crumbed and simply shake until coated. This works well in general, but be careful with fragile foods such as some flaky white fish fillets.
* British chef Gary Rhodes uses oatmeal for coating salmon. His glamorous presentation, ideal for dinner parties, involves dipping one side of the salmon in beaten egg and then coating the eggy side only with the oatmeal.

MIXED CRUMB COATINGS

Michelin-star calibre crumb coatings bear an astonishing resemblance to those produced in the home kitchen except that, with the inclusion of ingredients such as cornflakes, some of the chefs' output can seem more tacky than the coatings most good home cooks would be prepared to make. Also, the chefs aren't as determined to avoid deep-frying as the general public is. This simple mixture is used by British chef John Campbell for his cheese terrine.

SERVES 2

2 tbsp rolled oats

2 tbsp wheat flakes

2 tbsp fine white breadcrumbs

3 tbsp plain wheat-type flour

1 egg

2 tbsp milk

vegetable oil, for deep-frying

salt and pepper

Combine the oats, wheat flakes and breadcrumbs in a wide, shallow dish. Place the flour in a similar dish nearby and season it generously with salt and pepper. In another shallow dish, beat the egg and milk together until combined.

Dust each portion of food in the seasoned flour, making sure each is thoroughly coated. Dip into the egg wash, again turning to ensure it is thoroughly coated. Shake off any excess egg, then roll each portion in the grain mixture to coat evenly.

Place the coated food on a baking tray, cover and chill for 30–60 minutes before cooking.

Heat a pan of oil for deep-frying to 160°C/325°F. Fry the coated food in small batches until crisp and golden. Drain well and serve hot.

COOK'S NOTES

❊ The specific quantities of each grain product in this recipe are not as important as the ratios in which they're used. You simply need equal volumes of each. Scale the amounts up or down according to the quantity and size of food you wish to coat. The amount given here will cover 4 x 125g/4oz fish fillets or small chicken breasts. Be aware that the ratio of surface area to volume is an issue – if you beat the chicken breasts until flat, their exterior will be larger and therefore require more crumb mixture.

❊ If you would prefer to bake the crumbed food in the oven, omit the seasoned flour and egg. Instead, marinate the food as for grilled chicken (see page 160) so that the excess marinade gives the crumbs something to cling to, or coat the food in ice-cold plain yogurt. Bake at 190°C/375°F/Gas 5 for 20–60 minutes depending on what is being cooked – fish should not take long; chicken will take about an hour.

❊ If using chicken, turn it over halfway through baking.

❊ I like to add a little crushed allspice to crumb coating mixtures.

❊ Back in the day, John used this coating for a terrine of goats' and blue cheeses. Making it simply requires pressing together a selection of fresh mild goats' cheese, ash-covered goat cheese and Roquefort, all cubed, in a terrine mould for several hours. After slicing, coating and deep-frying, he would serve the morsels with a red bell pepper and chilli sorbet (seems a bit 2001 now!). A bought-in chilli, bell pepper and tomato relish or fresh-tasting chilli jam would work well too.

❊ You can use this basic egg-and-crumb method for quinoa. Boil the quinoa first, then drain and spread it out to dry thoroughly. In Martin Morales's *Ceviche* restaurant cookbook, prawns and asparagus are marinated in lime juice, then dipped in flour, egg and quinoa before deep-frying.

KASHA

Kasha means different things to different people. In shops today, the word is often used to denote ready-roasted buckwheat as opposed to raw buckwheat groats. Others use the term simply in place of buckwheat. According to Lesley Chamberlain's *The Food and Cooking of Eastern Europe*, however, kasha has traditionally referred to gruels and porridges, often made with buckwheat but also with millet or barley. Some people routinely toss the buckwheat in beaten egg before frying, which helps to keep the grains separate in the finished dish.

PER PERSON

½ tbsp vegetable oil, butter or duck fat
50g/2oz buckwheat groats
about 175ml/6fl oz chicken, fish, meat or
    vegetable stock
salt and pepper

Heat the oil, butter or duck fat in a saucepan. Add the buckwheat and cook, stirring, for 5 minutes or until the grains become orangey brown in colour and fragrant.

Pour in the stock and bring to the boil. Reduce the heat and simmer for 12–15 minutes or until the liquid is absorbed and the buckwheat is just tender.

Fluff up the grains with a fork and season to taste before further use or serving.

COOK'S NOTES

✳ To make a salad, add a handful of flat-leaf parsley leaves, 10 torn mint leaves, 2 chopped spring onions, 5cm/2in deseeded and sliced cucumber, plus a squeeze of lemon juice and salt and pepper to taste.
✳ While the buckwheat is cooking, sauté 2 thick rashers of bacon, finely chopped, in a little oil or butter. Stir into the cooked buckwheat with 2 finely chopped spring onions and some parsley and chives.
✳ Make a stuffing for bream or other long, round white fish by cooking double the quantities given above. Stir in a finely chopped onion fried in butter, a chopped hard-boiled egg and some herbs such as parsley, dill, oregano and chives, then heat through. Stuff the fish, place in a baking tin, pour some melted butter over it and bake at 180°C/350°F/Gas 4 until the fish is done. Stir 2–3 tbsp soured cream into the cooking juices in the tin to make a sauce.
✳ Dean & Deluca have devised a fabulous potato gratin made using 5 times the quantity of ingredients given above, plus chicken stock. While the buckwheat is cooking, sauté 250g/8oz chopped mushrooms and a sliced garlic clove for 10 minutes. Finely slice 1kg/2lb potatoes and 250g/8oz onions. In a large greased baking dish, place a layer of potatoes, then scatter with the onions, mushrooms and buckwheat, seasoning as you go. Cover with the remaining potato. Pour 350ml/12fl oz double cream over, then top with grated fontina or Gruyère cheese. Bake at 180°C/350°F/Gas 4 for 1 hour or until the potatoes are tender. As they say, it might not be traditionally Swiss, but it should be!

SAVOURY MILLET CAKE

This fat pancake, from a book by Jean-Georges Vongerichten and credited to Didier Virot, is an extremely versatile side dish, but also something I like to serve as a snack, covered with sauces or cream and piquant toppings. With a little sweetening it could be fried in walnut-sized balls and served with fruit sauce.

SERVES 4

200g/7oz millet
450ml/¾ pint water
50g/2oz butter, diced
3 eggs
4 tbsp milk
1 tbsp vegetable oil, plus extra
    for brushing
salt and pepper

Place the millet in a small saucepan with the water and a little salt. Bring to the boil. Skim the surface, then cover, reduce the heat right down and cook for 20 minutes or until all the water has been absorbed.

Remove the pan from the heat and leave the millet to stand, covered, for 10 minutes. Meanwhile, heat the oven to 240°C/475°F/Gas 9.

Stir the butter into the hot millet so that it melts into the grain.

In a small bowl, beat the eggs lightly and add them to the millet along with the milk, some salt and plenty of freshly ground pepper. Mix to give a thick batter.

Place a small, ovenproof non-stick frying pan, or a flameproof dish, over a high heat on the stovetop. When it is very hot, add the oil. Then, when you can see the haze rising from the oil, spoon the batter into the pan. Smooth over the surface to shape it into a large, round cake.

Cook for 3 minutes or until the edges of the cake start to firm up and the underside is golden. Transfer the pan to the hot oven and bake for 5 minutes. Carefully brush the setting surface of the millet cake with oil, then continue cooking for 3–5 minutes or until it is firm on top but not dry.

When cooked, remove the pan from the oven and carefully invert the millet cake onto a large serving plate so that the crisp-fried golden side is uppermost.

COOK'S NOTES

✤ The original recipe in Jean-Georges's book, co-authored with American food writer Mark Bittman, uses 2 whole eggs and 2 egg yolks. I'm not one for saving and reusing egg whites, hence the alteration, which works fine.
✤ They advise that while this dish 'can be served with almost anything, it is especially good with stews. My favourite uses are with roast chicken and a sauce of reduced chicken stock, or simply smeared with mascarpone or thickened crème fraîche and topped with flakes of smoked or roast salmon – even honey-roast salmon bought ready-made at the supermarket.
✤ As long as you're careful, it is possible to leave the oven off, turn the half-cooked cake onto a plate and ease it back into the pan. This helps to give a crisp, moist finish.

SKIRLIE

The name 'skirl-in-the-pipes', as this moreish onion and oat mixture from Scotland is traditionally known, compares the sound of it sizzling in the frying pan to the whirring noise of bagpipes. The dish is a deconstructed white mealie pudding, made by frying the ingredients together rather than packing them into beef intestines to make sausages. I was most tempted to revisit it not through researching old recipes but by a picture of skirlie-stuffed roast lamb in Sue Lawrence's mouthwatering book *Scots Cooking*, a stylish, modern take on the subject.

SERVES 4–6

25g/1oz butter
2 tbsp olive or vegetable oil
1 onion or leek, finely chopped
100g/3½oz medium or coarse oatmeal
salt and pepper

In a large frying pan, melt the butter with the oil over a moderate heat. Add the onion or leek and reduce the heat right down. Cook, stirring often, for 10 minutes or until soft and golden.

Mix in the oatmeal and cook, stirring, until all the fat is absorbed. Add some more oatmeal if there seems to be too much oil in the pan.

Cook, stirring frequently, for another 8–10 minutes or until the mixture is well toasted. Season to taste with salt and pepper before serving.

COOK'S NOTES

* Traditionally, this would be made with melted beef suet, or meat or bacon dripping, in place of the butter and oil.
* Try serving skirlie sprinkled over buttery mashed potatoes, combined with swede, if desired, or, as Sue suggests, over roast game birds in place of fried breadcrumbs.
* To use the mixture as a stuffing for roast leg of lamb, first have your butcher tunnel-bone the joint for you. Prepare the skirlie and leave it to cool, then pack it firmly into the hole created in the meat when the bone was removed. Tie along the joint with string to keep it together. Roast at 220°C/425°F/Gas 7 for 20 minutes before reducing the oven to 190°C/375°F/Gas 5 and cooking for another hour to give medium/well-done lamb. Always remember to leave roast joints to rest for 15 minutes before carving.
* Cut the tops off some beefsteak or other large tomatoes and use a spoon to scoop out the seeds and flesh. Fill the tomatoes with the skirlie, adding some of the chopped flesh if a particularly juicy result is desired, then bake in a moderate oven for 10–15 minutes until piping hot. Sprinkle the tops with parsley and, if you like, gently peel away the curled skin from the tomatoes before serving.
* The skirlie mixture can also be packed into a pudding bowl or cloth and steamed to serve as a side dish.
* Diana Henry makes caramelized oats to serve over a salad of liquorice-flavoured beetroot and goats' cheese. It involves sautéing 20g pumpernickel or rye breadcrumbs and 5g rolled oats in 15g butter for 20 seconds, then adding 1 tsp demerara sugar and tossing until the sugar begins to caramelize. This would also be good as an alternative to Roast Carrots with Dill Granola (see page 120).

UPPMA

Here is an Indian-style treatment of millet that works well as part of a feast featuring several small dishes served together, especially one for vegetarians. The combination of whole spices, urad dal and curry leaves that flavours the dish at the start of cooking is typical of the Kerala region, though the recipe is not an authentic Indian one. I'm astonished that curry leaves are still not commonplace in Britain, given the national passion for Indian food. The leaves freeze very well, however, so it's convenient to buy a large bunch from a specialist grocer.

SERVES 8

3 tbsp vegetable oil or ghee
1 tsp mustard seeds
1 tsp cumin seeds
1 tsp urad dal lentils
1 small dried red chilli
a few curry leaves
2 green chillies, sliced
1 medium onion, finely chopped
2.5cm/1in cube fresh root ginger, finely chopped
1 red bell pepper, chopped
75g/3oz broccoli, chopped
400g/13oz millet
700ml water
10g packed coriander leaves
salt and pepper

In a large pot, heat the oil or ghee, then stir in the mustard and cumin seeds, urad dal, dried red chilli and curry leaves. When the mustard seeds begin to pop, add the green chillies, onion and ginger and cook over a medium to low heat, stirring frequently, for 10 minutes or until the onion is well softened.

Add the red pepper, broccoli, millet and some salt and pepper. Continue cooking and stirring for another few minutes until the millet is slightly toasted, then pour in the water. Bring to the boil, cover the pan with a lid and simmer gently for 20 minutes or until the water has all been absorbed and the millet is puffed, fluffy and tender.

Stir in the coriander leaves and season the mixture to taste with salt and pepper. Fork through the millet and serve hot.

COOK'S NOTES

- Don't hesitate to use only the crunchy stalks of the broccoli in this dish, and save the florets for another recipe where their attractive appearance will make a difference.
- Swap other vegetables for the broccoli and red pepper, as desired. A few handfuls of spinach stirred in towards the end of cooking would be good; don't put it in any earlier or it will become slimy.
- This recipe will work fine with long-grain white rice or quinoa, or with bulgur wheat.
- Dried beans or lentils, cooked separately and stirred in towards the end of cooking, would turn this into a complete, one-bowl meal.
- You could also serve it alongside simple lemony grilled white fish, the paler oily fishes such as marlin and kingklip or chicken. Tandoori or tikka chicken and fish would also work well.

PUMPKIN AND SAGE PUDDING

There was an old *Spitting Image* series of sketches in which the grey puppet version of former British prime minister John Major would say 'Nice peas, Norma' to his wife at dinner every evening in a pathetic attempt to start conversation. In Australia we do a similar thing, observing after a long period of silence: 'That's a nice, dry bit of pumpkin.' Strongly flavoured dry pumpkin is what we like and is the best choice for this recipe. Butternut squash is just not as good. This recipe is based on one from the Italian food writer Emanuela Stucchi.

SERVES 4–6

100g/3½oz butter, plus extra for greasing

300g/10oz firm pumpkin flesh, peeled and deseeded

75g/3oz rolled oats

2 tbsp finely chopped sage

120g/4oz plain wheat-type flour

½ tsp baking powder

2 eggs, beaten

2 tbsp milk

salt and pepper

Heat oven to 180°C/350°F/Gas 4. Grease an ovenproof baking dish. Using a food processor, grate the pumpkin into fine shreds.

In a large frying pan or saucepan, melt the butter and add the grated pumpkin, rolled oats and sage. Cook over a moderate heat for about 10 minutes, stirring frequently. Set aside to cool.

Combine the flour, baking powder and some salt and pepper in a large mixing bowl. Make a well in the centre and add the eggs and milk. Beat lightly, gradually incorporating the flour to make a batter.

Stir in the cooked pumpkin and oats, then transfer the mixture to the greased oven dish and bake for 30 minutes or until firm. Serve hot.

COOK'S NOTES

* Root vegetables, including carrot, swede and parsnip, can be used in place of pumpkin. Vary the herbs according to your personal tastes, but choose robust varieties such as parsley, thyme, oregano, marjoram and rosemary.
* This pudding can be served as a side dish with chicken in various forms. A classy presentation is to use it as a base for roast chicken and a sauce of intense reduced stock or demi-glace.
* Vegetarians will enjoy it as part of a main meal, served, for example, with some cheese and a salad of broad beans and asparagus, or a sauté of peas, onion and lettuce.
* This pudding also makes a nice savoury teatime treat or snack, and is a welcome addition to a cooked breakfast with eggs and fish or ham.
* Replacing the rolled oats with flakes of other grains is an option but not quite as successful because oats have a special creamy flavour and texture. Wheat flakes are the best second choice. Barley and rye are okay but very dry. You could, of course, combine any of the above for a mixed-grain version.

BRAISED BARLEY WITH LEMON AND SPICES

Preserved lemons and other bright-tasting aromatics here lift what are normally considered to be two very humble ingredients – barley and celery – out of the ordinary. Europeans rarely cook with their cultivated variety of celery, regarding it as a salad vegetable. However, braising is an excellent treatment for it, and easy to boot. When you lift the lid off the oven dish and give the mixture a brief stir before serving, in addition to smelling the wonderful fragrance, you will see it has become luxuriously creamy and comforting, quite like a risotto.

SERVES 2-4

275ml/9fl oz vegetable, chicken
   or lamb stock
50g/2oz semi-pearled or pot barley
6 celery sticks, chopped
1 piece of preserved lemon zest, chopped
2 tbsp lemon juice
1 tbsp olive oil
4–6 sprigs of thyme, or a bunch of
   parsley and coriander stalks
1 bay leaf
10 peppercorns, crushed
10 coriander seeds, crushed
1 garlic clove, crushed
a pinch of chilli flakes

Heat the oven to 180°C/350°F/Gas 4. Put all the ingredients in a casserole. Cover and bake in the hot oven for 1½ hours or until the barley is tender and most of the liquid has been absorbed.

Remove the casserole dish from the oven and stir the mixture briefly to combine the ingredients. Pick out the large flavourings before serving.

COOK'S NOTES

❋ This dish is a good accompaniment to roast or grilled chicken and lamb (see pages 160–1). Vegetarians will be happy to eat it as a main course.

❋ For a simple British barley braise to serve with roast meat, combine the barley, celery, bay and thyme in a casserole with 300ml/½ pint lamb stock and cook as instructed here.

❋ Also suitable for this recipe are black barley, plump wholegrain rice, freekeh and semi-pearled wheatberries such as farro. Polished short- or medium-grain rice would be good too, but cut the cooking time and quantity of stock a little.

❋ This dish can be quite fiery, depending on the size of your 'pinch' of chilli flakes. If your tolerance to heat is low, a few flakes will do.

❋ Preserved lemon is a lovely inclusion, but feel free to skip it if you have none to hand.

❋ When using preserved lemons, trim away the flesh of the fruit and use the zest only. People cut up lemons for preserving in different ways. Here '1 piece' of preserved lemon zest means about a quarter of what would have been a whole lemon, or you could use all the zest of a baby preserved lemon as sold under the Belazu label.

❋ The stock and preserved lemons make this dish salty enough; there's no need to add more.

KOREAN GRAINS AND BEANS

This dish, known as ogokbap, comes via Marc Millon, author, with wife Kim (who is a food photographer), of the intriguing *Flavours of Korea*. They spent much time travelling in this little-known country and feature many recipes from Marc's Korean grandmother, including several that mix rice with other grains. While this was a common means of stretching the rice supply, Marc says that this dish 'is by no means a poor person's rice, but a very special and splendid one'. Fans of Jamaican red beans and rice or 'Moors and Christians' will love this dish.

SERVES 8–10

50g/2oz dried black kidney beans
50g/2oz dried small red beans or aduki beans
200g/7oz medium-grain white rice
100g/3½oz sticky rice
50g/2oz white pearled barley
50g/2oz millet

Soak the black and red beans together in a bowl of water for 3–4 hours.

Meanwhile, wash the 2 rices thoroughly. Place them in a separate bowl with the barley and millet, then cover them with water and soak for 2 hours.

In a pan of fresh boiling water, cook the beans for 30–45 minutes or until tender. Drain, reserving the cooking liquid, and set aside. Next drain all the grains, discarding their soaking liquid.

Put the beans and all the grains in a heavy pot. Measure the bean cooking liquid in a measuring jug and make it up to 800ml with fresh water. Add this to the pot and bring to the boil. Give it a stir, then reduce the heat, cover and simmer for 30 minutes until the water is absorbed and the grains are tender.

COOK'S NOTES

- Korean grocers often sell bags of mixed grains featuring whole rather than refined rices, plus peas and pulses ready to cook. The pack I have in my kitchen includes an astonishing range: barley, millet, 2 types of brown rice, black sticky rice, Job's tears, red and black beans, mung beans, dried corn and dried peas. The problem is getting the pulses to cook as quickly as the rice. That's not an issue with this recipe because here the beans are cooked first.
- There is no salt or any flavourings used in this dish, in the expectation that it will accompany strong-tasting, saucy main dishes that are very likely to be made with soy sauce. Add salt if you like, but not to the beans while they are cooking, as this will toughen them.
- If your barley is semi-pearled and beige rather than polished until white, you will need to preboil it for about 15 minutes before combining it with the rice and beans in the pot. If you don't, the rice will disintegrate before the barley is cooked.

ROAST CARROTS WITH DILL GRANOLA

Although this fun savoury granola is brow-raisingly moreish, I've deliberately kept the quantities small. Without the fresh dill, it can be stored for weeks in an airtight container and is readily varied, but ultimately it's a condiment for sprinkling – like Parmesan cheese, gremolata or pangrattato – and there is only so much you will ever need. It's easy to knock out a fresh batch, unlike making a breakfast cereal where larger quantities and more sticky sweetener enhance the feeling that's it's a chore.

SERVES 4

400g/13 oz even-sized carrots
olive oil spray, for roasting

For the dill granola
50g/2oz rolled oats
1 heaped tbsp pine kernels
1 heaped tbsp flaked almonds
2 tsp maple syrup
1 large garlic clove, thinly sliced
2 tbsp olive oil
1 tbsp chopped dill
salt and pepper

Preheat the oven to 180°C/350°F/Gas 4. To make the dill granola, combine the rolled oats, pine kernels, flaked almonds, maple syrup, garlic and olive oil in a bowl. Add plenty of salt and pepper and mix well.

Spread the mixture on a baking tray and bake for 15 minutes, stirring every 5 minutes, until golden. Remove from the oven and tip into a bowl or storage box to cool (you don't want to scorch the granola on the residual heat of the baking tray).

Trim the carrots to the desired size. Spritz the baking tray with oil and place the carrots on it. Spritz the carrots with oil and season with salt and pepper. Roast for 20–25 minutes, depending on size, turning halfway through cooking.

Put the carrots on a serving dish. Take 3–4 tablespoons of granola and stir the chopped dill into it. Sprinkle the mixture over the carrots and serve.

COOK'S NOTES

❋ I like the luxurious quality of pine kernels, but this is an ideal opportunity to use seeds such as sunflower or pumpkin. You can also swap the syrup for another sweetener such as honey or agave.

❋ Replace the dill with other fresh herbs such as tarragon or basil. You want something tender but assertive – chives are a waste of time here because of the strength of the garlic. Freshly grated lemon zest is a wonderful last-minute inclusion too.

❋ For a larger vegetable side dish, cut 2 red onions into wedges and roast them alongside the carrots. Alternatively, replace the carrots with tomato halves, which should only take around 15 minutes in the oven. The granola would also work with a salad of roast pumpkin and rocket.

AFRICAN CORN AND PEANUT PATTIES

Africans use a wide variety of dark greens in the manner of spinach. The terms morogo and African spinach cover a group of leaves that may include those from pumpkin and sweet potato plants, as well as silverbeet and edible wild greens such as buffalo-thorn. Peanuts, or groundnuts, are technically not nuts at all but the seeds of a legume similar to the soya bean. They are characteristic of West African cuisine, having been taken there from their native South America by the Portuguese. Ironically, it was the Africans who took them to the USA.

SERVES 2-4

50g/2oz samp or hominy
75g/3oz coarse cornmeal
150g/5oz spinach leaves, shredded
¼ tsp ground turmeric
¼ tsp salt
a sprinkle of chilli flakes
275ml/9fl oz boiling water
25g/1oz chopped roasted and salted peanuts
plain wheat-type flour, for dusting
a little butter and olive or vegetable oil, for frying
pepper

Soak the samp or hominy in a bowl of cold water overnight or for at least 4 hours. Drain and rinse.

In a large, heavy saucepan, combine the soaked corn, the cornmeal, spinach, turmeric, salt and chilli flakes. Stir in the boiling water and place the saucepan over a low heat. Cook, stirring frequently, for 20–30 minutes, adding more hot water to the pan as necessary.

When the mixture is very thick, remove it from the heat. Stir in the peanuts and pepper to taste. Set aside until the mixture is cool enough to handle. Shape it into patties using floured hands, then fry in a little butter and oil until browned on both sides. Serve hot with a chilli tomato sauce or relish as desired (see Cook's Notes).

COOK'S NOTES

❖ Instead of shaping the mixture into patties, you could leave it soft and serve it as a textured alternative to cornmeal dishes such as polenta.
❖ The corn and nuts complement each other to form a complete protein dish, so this recipe can be used as the base of a vegetarian meal.
❖ Serve with a bright-tasting, chilli-laden tomato sauce or relish, with or without some barbecued meats and poultry. The tomato sauce layered with cornmeal to make Layered Cornmeal with Spicy Tomato Sauce (see page 85) would be a lovely accompaniment.

FARRO WITH CHESTNUTS AND CAVOLO NERO

Based on a dish enjoyed one winter at Salt Yard, where it was served as a tapa, this recipe is too easy to save for special occasions. Vacuum-packed chestnuts have great taste benefits over canned and offer so much convenience over dried chestnuts that they seem to have knocked them off the shelves of health food shops altogether. Although technically nuts (and the lowest-calorie ones at that), chestnuts compositionally have more in common with starchy vegetables and their impressive list of nutritional benefits includes B-complex vitamins, vitamin C, folates, fibre and iron.

SERVES 4

200g/7oz farro
2 branches cavolo nero, about 16 large leaves
2 tbsp olive oil
2 large banana shallots, finely chopped
200g/7oz small chestnut mushrooms, sliced
180ml/6fl oz stock
12 vacuum-packed chestnuts, cooked and
    peeled
salt and pepper

Rinse the farro and cook it in a generous quantity of salted boiling water until almost tender – the time needed will depend on the type of farro (whole, semi-pearled, quick-cook) and you should reduce the suggested cooking time on the pack by a couple of minutes. Drain in a sieve, refresh under cold running water and set aside to drain thoroughly.

Meanwhile, cut the leaves of the cavolo nero into ribbons and blanch them in another pan of salted boiling water for 1 minute.

In a frying pan or casserole, heat the olive oil and fry the shallots until soft. Add the sliced mushrooms and cook, stirring, until they are browned.

Tip the farro and cavolo nero into the pan, pour in the stock and add the chestnuts. Add plenty of salt and pepper, then toss together until most of the liquid has been absorbed. Taste and adjust the seasoning before serving.

COOK'S NOTES

✲ Replace the farro with spelt, Kamut, barley, whole oats or buckwheat and vary the stock (vegetable, mushroom, chicken etc.) according to how you plan to serve it.
✲ The meatiness of the mushrooms and chestnuts means you could eat this on its own, or topped with a poached egg, for a Zen-Mediterranean lunch or supper. However, it is an excellent all-in-one accompaniment to roast chicken or pheasant and also works with some sausages.
✲ Button mushrooms or something fancier are equally welcome here or you can leave out the mushrooms altogether if desired. Swap the cavolo nero for kale, hispi cabbage or leaves of Savoy. Spring greens would work too.

CORN ICE CREAM

A favourite in our household, this unusual ice cream is reminiscent of good creamy rich vanilla but has an other-worldly taste that unknowing guests tend not to be able to place. The secret of success, I've decided, having made many batches using several different recipes and techniques, is not actually the corn but the degree of straining the mixture receives before churning. Results are transformed when the mixture is put through a chinois fin, which is a fine-meshed conical sieve, pushing down on the solids but not forcing them through.

MAKES 750ML/1¼ PINTS

2 sweetcorn cobs, husks and strings
    removed
675ml/1¼ pints milk
2 tsp vanilla extract
3 egg yolks
200g/7oz caster sugar
2 tbsp liquid glucose
225ml/7½fl oz double cream

Using a large knife, cut the corn kernels from the cobs. Scrape the cobs with the back of the knife to squeeze out as much of the kernels and 'milk' as possible. Place the kernels and their liquid in a food processor with the milk and vanilla extract and purée until smooth. Transfer to a large saucepan and bring to the boil.

Meanwhile, in a large mixing bowl, whisk the egg yolks and sugar together until smooth. Gradually add a few ladles of the simmering milk mixture to the yolk mixture, stirring to combine.

Add the thinned yolk mixture to the saucepan of simmering milk and cook over a medium to low heat for 6–8 minutes or until the custard is thick enough to coat the back of a spoon. Turn off the heat and stir in the liquid glucose. Set aside to cool completely.

When the custard has cooled, whip the cream in a large mixing bowl until stiff peaks form. Strain the corn custard using a very fine-meshed sieve and gently fold it into the whipped cream. Chill the mixture thoroughly if necessary and churn in an ice cream machine according to the manufacturer's instructions.

COOK'S NOTES

✽ Once you have used liquid glucose for ice cream, you will clearly see the difference in quality it makes and will want to use it all the time.
✽ Mark Miller of Sante Fe's Coyote Café fame uses ground coriander as well as vanilla to flavour his recipe for corn ice cream. It really is delicious, as is the use of ground cumin. You only need to add ¼ tsp or so to the mixture.
✽ You would think, wouldn't you, having learned of the flavour to be extracted from corn cobs in vegetable stock (see page 51) that adding them to the simmering milk mixture would boost the flavour of this ice cream. In fact, I have found it can take it a little OTT and you are better off retaining the trimmed cobs for making stock instead.
✽ Accompaniments based on dark chocolate, or oranges, are particularly good with this.

MILLET AND GRAPE CLAFOUTIS

Although it is most commonly made with cornmeal these days, milhassou is a type of old Spanish and French country pudding traditionally made (the name is a clue) from millet. This grape-studded custard-and-clafoutis-style version tastes strongly of honey and lemon and, as it is rich with eggs and milk, smoothes over any bitter taste that may be present in the millet flour. It makes a good Sunday lunch dessert or, when cooked in ramekins, a comforting one to eat on a Sunday evening in front of the television.

SERVES 6

150g/5oz seedless grapes
2 tbsp brandy or eau de vie
butter, for greasing
600ml/1 pint milk
4 eggs
75g/3oz millet flour
250g/8oz runny honey
finely grated zest of 1 lemon

Place the grapes in a mixing bowl and cover with the alcohol. Set aside to marinate for about 1 hour.

Heat the oven to 220°C/425°F/Gas 7. Grease 6 small ovenproof ramekins or soufflé dishes of about 250ml/8fl oz capacity and divide the marinated grapes among them.

In a heavy saucepan, slowly bring the milk to scalding point. Meanwhile, in a mixing bowl, whisk together the eggs, millet flour, honey and lemon zest. When the milk is hot, slowly pour it over the egg mixture, whisking constantly.

Pour the custard mixture into the ramekins, whisking again briefly after you pour each one to ensure the millet is evenly distributed. Put them on a baking tray and cook for 10–12 minutes until only just set and golden. Eat warm or cold.

COOK'S NOTES

* Replace the grapes with fruit such as cherries, berries or sliced plums and nectarines if desired. Alternatively, you can omit the fruit and alcohol altogether if you prefer, and use orange zest in place of lemon.
* Instead of dividing the mixture among individual ramekins, cook it as one large pudding for 20 minutes at the same temperature.
* Some of the millet will sink in the oven to form a thin layer at the base of the ramekin. You don't want this to be thick, which is why it is important to whisk the custard mixture after it has been poured into the ramekins. For this, I prefer to use straight-sided ramekins.
* The strength and nature of the honey flavour will vary according to the individual variety you choose.
* As ever, the fresher the millet flour, the better the result. You can also make this pudding using coarsely ground cornmeal, sorghum flour or with wheat semolina. Coconut flour, which gives a sturdier texture, is a good option too.

STICKY BLACK RICE CUSTARD

Although it is sometimes called glutinous rice, sticky black rice does not contain gluten; no rices do. I love these elegant long grains with their variegated colours, but sticky black rice does not seem to be versatile enough to warrant stocking in major supermarkets – most recipes simply involve boiling it with sugar and coconut milk one way or another. And while it has a lovely flavour and texture, it can lend a pinky-grey hue to ingredients it is cooked with, as is the case here. Simply close your eyes and think of Thailand.

SERVES 4–6

50g/2oz butter
100g/3½oz sticky black rice
340ml/12fl oz coconut milk
125ml/4fl oz milk
100g/3½oz caster sugar
1 vanilla pod, split
3 egg yolks
4–6 tbsp desiccated coconut

Melt 15g/½oz butter in a large, heavy saucepan over a moderate heat. Add the rice and stir to coat. Add the coconut milk, milk and sugar and stir to combine. Scrape the seeds from the inside of the vanilla pod and add them to the pan along with the pod. Bring the mixture to the boil, then reduce the heat and cook gently for 10 minutes.

In a large mixing bowl, whisk the egg yolks. Add a ladle of the hot milk mixture to the yolks and whisk to combine. Pour the yolk mixture into the saucepan of milk mixture, stirring constantly, and cook for 2 minutes. Stir in the remaining butter. The mixture will be very thick.

Pour into a serving dish and set aside to cool. Cover the cooled custard with clingfilm to prevent a skin forming and chill for 2 hours. Meanwhile, in a heavy frying pan, toast the coconut over a medium to low heat for 2–3 minutes, stirring constantly, until the coconut is fragrant and has an even golden brown colour. Immediately tip the toasted coconut into a small bowl and set aside to cool.

When ready to serve, cover the black rice custard with an even layer of the toasted coconut.

COOK'S NOTES

✻ This dish can be made with hominy corn in place of the sticky black rice.
✻ It's rich but moreish – rather too so. Serve it plainly and in small portions. If you think you must add something else, choose simple fresh fruit from the tropics such as mango and use the black rice (or corn) custard almost like a scoop of ice cream served on the side.
✻ For a vegan pudding, make the traditional Thai dessert kao neow dahm. Simmer 200g/7oz sticky black rice in 250ml coconut milk and 500ml water for about 45 minutes or until tender, adding more water towards the end if the grains need to simmer longer. If you have a pandan leaf to hand, bundle it up and throw it in at the beginning. When the rice is done, stir in 3 tbsp palm sugar and ½ tsp salt (or more to taste), then serve topped with toasted coconut flakes, a few slices of banana and maybe some extra coconut cream if liked.

BANANA AND COCONUT PUDDING

It's astonishing that such a healthy dessert – made from fresh fruit and cooked in a steamer – could taste so rich and luxurious. The deceptively decadent creaminess comes from mashed or puréed fruit. This very simple recipe is based on a traditional Indian pudding introduced to me by Das Sreedharan of Rasa Restaurants, who in turn got it from a Keralan home cook called Mrs Nair who made it for Onam celebrations. We don't often see steamed dishes in Indian restaurants or books aimed at the Western market, but they are part of the cuisine.

SERVES 4

3 tbsp millet

4 large, very ripe bananas

50g/2oz palm sugar or jaggery,
    grated if necessary

1 vanilla pod, or 1 tsp vanilla extract

4 heaped tbsp coconut flakes or chips

In a small saucepan of boiling water, cook the millet for 12–15 minutes or until tender.

Meanwhile, mash or purée the bananas with the palm sugar or jaggery. Split open the vanilla pod, if using, and scrape all the seeds into the banana mixture; otherwise, stir in the vanilla extract.

Fill a steamer with water and bring to the boil.

Drain the millet thoroughly and spread it out on a tray or plate to dry a little. Then stir the millet into the sweetened banana mixture until it is well combined.

Spoon the mixture into heatproof serving bowls or cups and top each with a heaped tablespoon of coconut. If liked, add a small piece of vanilla pod to each serving as a decoration.

Cover each pudding with a piece of foil (this is vital) and place in the steamer for 15 minutes. Carefully remove the hot foil from the cooked puddings and serve hot or warm.

COOK'S NOTES

* In Das's home state of Kerala, this pudding would be made from sago rather than millet and a significant amount of white sugar in addition to the jaggery. Soft ripe jackfruit is sometimes used in place of banana.
* The basic recipe can be made with puréed mango or berries, or a thick sauce of dried apricots. Whatever your choice, you'll need around 500g/1lb prepared fruit to cook with.
* When varying the grains, think first of the pearly whites: quinoa, polished rice or indeed sago and tapioca – these two only require a brief soak in cold water before being combined with the banana. You can also make this pudding with chia, in which case stir the seeds into the sweetened fruit mixture, then leave it to stand for 30 minutes before putting it in the ramekins and steaming.
* Freshly grated coconut is delicious and authentic here, but you can also make this dish using dried shredded coconut or desiccated coconut. In the case of the latter, use a little less.
* The dessert looks terrific steamed and presented in foil parcels, or banana leaves if they're available. Dip the banana leaves in hot water before use to make them easy to fold into parcels, and have ready thin strips of leaf or kitchen string to hold them together.
* If you choose an unstarchy fruit, you could consider serving the puddings with a spoonful of lightly sweetened cream, some rich yogurt or good-quality coconut cream.

OATMEAL PRALINE ICE CREAM

This richly flavoured ice cream is based on one in food writer Sue Lawrence's *Scots Cooking*. Although the liquid glucose is incorporated in the praline mixture rather than the custard base, the ice cream still has a scoopable texture. It's quite intense, so small servings are all that are needed. Sue serves it with a hot sauce of melted Dundee marmalade and a dash of whisky.

SERVES 6–8

500ml/17fl oz milk
300ml/½ pint double cream
2 eggs
125g/4oz caster sugar

For the praline
vegetable oil, for greasing
150g/5oz pinhead or medium oatmeal
140g/4½oz liquid glucose
125g/4oz caster sugar

COOK'S NOTES

✣ In her recipe, Sue uses 4 large egg yolks rather than 2 whole eggs. She also admits that if you're feeling lazy you could simply stir the ground oat praline into some softened bought vanilla ice cream.

✣ Serve on its own or with a few berries. You could use a warm berry compote (see page 163).

✣ This is an excellent custard base that can be used for other ice creams. An interesting grainy one from Germany is made by blending 125g/4oz dark pumpernickel breadcrumbs into the cooled custard before churning.

✣ To make vanilla custard sauce, add a scraped vanilla pod and its seeds while heating the milk and cream, and continue with this recipe until the custard thickens.

Put the milk and cream in a heavy saucepan and slowly bring to scalding point. Meanwhile, in a bowl, whisk the eggs and sugar together until smooth. Pour the hot milk over the egg mixture, stirring constantly.

Return the custard to the saucepan and place over a low heat. Cook, stirring constantly, until it has the consistency of double cream – this will take about 10 minutes. The custard will thicken on cooling. Set it aside to cool, stirring frequently to prevent a skin forming.

To make the praline, oil a baking sheet. Place the oatmeal in a heavy, dry frying pan and toast, stirring constantly, for 2–3 minutes until the oatmeal is fragrant and browned. Tip it onto the oiled baking sheet and set aside.

In a small, heavy saucepan, combine the liquid glucose and sugar and cook over a low heat, stirring constantly, until the sugar dissolves. Use a pastry brush dipped in cold water to brush down any sugar stuck to the side of the pan.

When the sugar has dissolved, stop stirring and raise the heat a little. Simmer for 8–10 minutes or until golden brown, swirling the pan occasionally. Pour the caramel over the oatmeal, ensuring most of it is covered. Set aside to cool.

When set, break up the oatmeal praline and place it in a food processor, setting aside some larger chunks to serve. Pulse to give coarse crumbs.

Stir the praline into the cold custard and transfer the mixture to an ice cream machine. Churn until frozen. Let it soften for 20 minutes before serving, scattered with the reserved chunks of praline.

BUCKWHEAT, CACAO AND APRICOT ICE-CREAM SANDWICHES

Alice Medrich's fabulous buckwheat butter cookies from her book *Pure Dessert* became known as 'nibby biscuits' in our home. They are made with cacao nibs – pieces of hulled cacao beans – rather than the usual choc chips and make a crisp lacy cookie of sophisticated flavour.

MAKES 20

For the cookies
225g/7½oz unsalted butter, softened
100g/3½oz caster sugar
¼ tsp salt
40g/1½oz cacao nibs
1½ tsp vanilla extract
160g/5½oz plain wheat-type flour
75g/3oz buckwheat flour

For the ice-cream sandwiches
600ml/1 pint vanilla ice cream
300g/10oz apricot jam

Using an electric mixer, cream the butter, sugar and salt together in a large mixing bowl until creamy. Add the cacao nibs and vanilla on low speed, then the plain and buckwheat flours and turn off the machine as soon as they are incorporated.

Bring the dough together with a scraper and knead briefly before shaping into a cylinder 5cm/2in in diameter. Wrap in clingfilm and refrigerate for 2–12 hours.

When ready to cook, heat the oven to 180°C/350°F/Gas 4 and line 2 baking sheets with baking parchment. Use a sharp knife to cut the chilled log of dough into 5mm/¼in slices. Lay them at least 4cm/1½in apart on the lined baking sheet, as they will spread in the oven.

Bake for 12–15 minutes, turning halfway through cooking, until the cookies are pale gold at the edges – do not let them brown even at the perimeters, as this will make them too crumbly to sandwich. Transfer the baking parchment with the cookies still on it to a wire rack and leave to cool. The cookies can be stored in an airtight container for a month or more.

To make the ice-cream sandwiches, allow the ice cream to soften for 1 hour in the fridge. Match the cookies in similarly shaped pairs. Gently spread 2 tbsp ice cream on the flat side of one cookie so that it comes 5mm/¼in from the edge. Swirl 1 tbsp apricot jam through it and sandwich with a matching cookie.

COOK'S NOTES

- You could get away with cheap ice cream and jam here, but using best-quality vanilla and a small-batch apricot preserve such as that from Mary's Marmalade (which contains the kernels) will give a haute cuisine result for comparatively little extra cost.
- Swap the apricot jam for morello cherry or raspberry if preferred.
- Alice Medrich suggests serving the cookies alongside blackberry sorbet, or making them into linzer hearts (a bit like Jammie Dodgers) with blackberry jam.
- For a nutritional boost, you can add chia seeds and/or whole buckwheat groats to the dough. Chopped dried cherries are good if you like some fruit in a cookie, but remember the texture of the baked dough is crunchy rather than chewy and, although fine, such additions make no particular improvement here.
- If you specifically want to use raw cacao nibs, check that the label states that they are raw. Sometimes the slightly different term 'cocoa nibs' is used to specify the roasted product.

BAKED CARAMEL APPLES WITH SPELT

You know all those low-cal, low-fat recipes for baked apples? The depressing sort with artificial sweetener and a dollop of zero-flavour yogurt? This isn't anything like those – it's a proper homely, rib-sticking, country comfort sort of dessert that will look all the better if you serve it wearing an apron. Having grown up in Australia, my default cooking apple is a Granny Smith, rather than the English favourite, the Bramley. The not-too-sweet Granny Smith's size is more amenable to individual servings and the flesh doesn't disintegrate on cooking.

SERVES 4

50g/2oz pearled spelt
4 Granny Smith apples
50g/2oz walnuts, chopped
50g/2oz raisins or sultanas
50g/2oz dark muscovado sugar
50g/2oz butter, plus extra for greasing
125ml/4fl oz apple juice, sherry or brandy
double cream or custard, to serve

Put the spelt in a small saucepan and cover generously with water. Simmer for 15 minutes until the grains are almost tender, then drain and refresh under cold running water.

Heat the oven to 180°C/350°F/Gas 4. Remove the apple cores and score the skin around the middle of each fruit. Place them in a lightly greased ovenproof dish.

Mix the walnuts, raisins, sugar, butter and half the cooked spelt together. Use this mixture to firmly stuff the apples, letting it spill out over the top. Spoon the remainder of the spelt around the base of the baking dish and pour in the apple juice or alcohol.

Bake for 30 minutes, basting occasionally, then remove from the oven and leave to stand for 10 minutes before serving with cream or custard.

COOK'S NOTES

✲ If you prefer a spicier flavour, add 1–2 tsp ground cinnamon, ginger and/or mixed spice. You can also stud each apple with 3 cloves – this gives a great flavour, but do remember to remove them before serving.
✲ Finely grated lemon and orange zests make good additions to the filling.
✲ Instead of spelt, you could use farro, Kamut, pearl barley or whole oats and adjust the parboiling period accordingly. Pecans or chopped whole almonds are the best alternative nuts.
✲ The amount of liquid you'll need will vary according to the size of your baking dish. Don't choose one so big that it spreads out and evaporates rapidly in the oven; just a little space around the apples is ideal.

WHOLEMEAL PASTRY CASE

As with wholemeal noodles, texture is – almost – all when it comes to wholemeal pastry. It is not the flavour of the complete grain that people sometimes object to, but the unfortunate tendency the resulting dough has in many cooks' hands to seem like wet cardboard as it is being chewed. The increasing acceptance that wholegrain foods are essential to optimum health means that good wholewheat flours are now quite easy to buy, and even supermarkets sell a variety of types, including superfine grinds specifically for pastry making.

MAKES A 23CM/9IN TART CASE

300g/10oz superfine wholemeal
   wheat-type flour, plus extra for dusting
1 tsp salt
150g/5oz butter, finely diced
4–5 tbsp water
1 egg yolk (optional)

Sift the flour and salt into a bowl. Add the butter and rub in until the mixture resembles fine breadcrumbs. Make a well in the centre, then quickly work in the water and the egg yolk, if using, to make a dough. Roll into a ball, cover with clingfilm and place in the fridge for at least 30 minutes.

Heat the oven to 190°C/375°F/Gas 5 and place a baking sheet in the oven. Roll out the pastry on a lightly floured work surface until 3mm/1/8in thick. Lay the pastry over the tart tin and gently lift, ease and press it down into the corners of the tin, letting the excess hang. Prick the base with a fork.

Line the pastry with a large sheet of baking parchment and weigh the paper down with dried beans. Bake on the hot baking sheet for 10 minutes. Remove the paper and beans, then trim off the excess pastry with a knife. Return to the oven for a further 5 minutes. Cool before filling.

COOK'S NOTES

✻ Breadmaking flour is not ideal for pastry making because it is strong in gluten. Packs of flour specifically labelled as suitable for pastry making are made from wheats that are low in gluten so that the dough does not become too elastic or difficult to roll. Yet it is the low level of gluten required for pastry making that makes it simple to switch all or half the quantity of wheat flour in this recipe for other varieties of grain with relative confidence.

✻ If the wholemeal flour you have to hand includes substantial pieces of wheat bran, don't worry. Use this tip from Clare Marriage of Doves Farm: sift the flour to separate the bran and make your pastry with the resulting fine flour. Then scatter the bran over the base of the lined tart tin so that it will combine with the filling. You'll eat the healthy bran, but the texture of the pastry will also be pleasing.

✻ Vegetarian cookery expert Sarah Brown includes 1/2 tsp baking powder in her wholemeal pastry recipe to give further lightness to the dough. She also uses 1 tbsp oil, she says, to keep the pastry moist without making it tough, and 1 tsp sugar (even in savoury tarts) to aid elasticity.

✻ Pastry that is studded with rolled oats tastes terrific. Use equal weights of plain wheat-type flour, rolled oats and butter and add an egg to the mixture if desired.

✻ Another option is to replace a proportion of the flour with finely ground nuts.

CHOCOLATE POLENTA SOUFFLE

On first reading this method of soufflé making, I was extremely dubious that it could work. Trying to fold egg whites, however stiffly beaten, into a tray of cooled and set cooked polenta was surely like trying to commit assault and battery with a tutu. In fact, it works very well, though a degree of experience and confidence in folding egg whites is helpful. Use a large metal spoon to help you cut a swathe through the polenta, but work with a light hand.

SERVES 4

400ml/14fl oz milk

50g/2oz stoneground cornmeal

2 tbsp unsweetened cocoa powder

1 tbsp vanilla extract or brandy

80g/3oz caster sugar, plus extra for dusting

40g/1½oz 100 per cent pure dark chocolate, grated

4 egg whites

butter, for greasing

sifted icing or powdered sugar, to decorate

Place the milk, cornmeal, cocoa, and vanilla or brandy in a large, heavy saucepan. Measure out the sugar and set aside 2 tbsp of it to mix into the egg whites later. Place the rest of the sugar in the pan.

Bring to the boil, stirring constantly to remove lumps. Reduce the heat to a very gentle simmer and cook the mixture, stirring often, for 25 minutes until thick and rich. Stir in the chocolate, then remove from the heat and set aside to cool.

Meanwhile, grease 4 x 250ml/8fl oz ramekins or soufflé dishes. Place some sugar in one and gently shake it around the interior of the dish to line with a thin film of crystals. Tap out the excess and repeat with the remaining dishes.

When the polenta has cooled, heat the oven to 200°C/400°F/ Gas 6. Whisk the egg whites in a large bowl until soft peaks form. Add the reserved 2 tbsp sugar and continue whisking until the whites form a stiff and glossy meringue.

Take a large spoonful of the meringue and stir it into the chocolate polenta mixture to help lighten it. Then repeat with another spoonful of meringue.

Gently fold the chocolate mixture into the bowl of meringue, carefully cutting and stirring the mixture until combined without squashing out the air bubbles in the meringue.

Divide the soufflé mixture among the prepared dishes. Place them together in a baking dish and fill the baking dish with water until the level reaches two-thirds up the sides of the ramekins or soufflé dishes. Bake for 25 minutes until risen and serve hot dusted with icing sugar.

COOK'S NOTES

❖ Use the leftover egg yolks to make vanilla custard sauce (see Cook's Notes, page 131) to serve.
❖ A tiny scoop of premium bought ice cream or sorbet from your best local supplier would make a refreshing accompaniment.
❖ If you can't buy 100 per cent pure dark chocolate, replace it with a slightly sweetened dark chocolate that has a high cocoa solids content, such as 70 per cent or over.
❖ Candied citron, if you can find some of good quality (there is a recipe on davidlebovitz.com), is a classic Italian flavouring for this dessert. Finely chop it and fold into the meringue along with the chocolate.

TEFF LEMON CREAM BARS

Here is further proof that almonds are a gluten-free flour's best friend – they mellow the grassy taste of brown teff flour in these delicious bars. A rich cream topping, like cheesecake without the cheese, puts them at the decadent end of teatime treats; they are also ideal served as a dessert with fresh berries. Choosing unwaxed lemons is important when you are using the zest. Those with thick, rough but unblemished skin are quickest and easiest to grate. For three large lemons it's worth getting out the electric juicer too.

SERVES 12

For the pastry

225g/7½oz salted butter, softened,
    plus extra for greasing
100g/3½oz caster sugar
1 egg
½ tsp almond extract
1 tbsp cornflour
200g/7oz ground almonds
200g/7oz teff flour
1 tsp xanthan gum
½ tsp salt

For the filling

50g/2oz coconut flour
600ml/1 pint double cream
300g/10oz caster sugar,
    plus extra for sprinkling
4 eggs
finely grated zest and juice of 3 large
    unwaxed lemons

In a large mixing bowl, cream the butter and sugar together or use an electric mixer. Beat in the egg and almond extract until combined, then sprinkle in the cornflour to halt any separation. Combine the remaining dry ingredients and gradually add them to the butter mixture to form a dough. Use a scraper to bring it all together, wrap in clingfilm and chill for a minimum of 2 hours.

You might want to make a start on zesting and juicing the lemons for the topping before you bake the pastry because it only requires 10–15 minutes in the oven.

Heat the oven to 180°C/350°F/Gas 4. Line a 20 x 25 x 5cm/ 8 x 10 x 2in baking tin with a double layer of foil, leaving enough overhang at the long sides to help you lift the cooked cake from the tin. Grease the foil lightly. Using sheets of baking parchment or plastic wrap to prevent sticking, roll half the pastry into a rectangle with a depth of 3mm/⅛in and lay it in the tin, trimming off the excess. Bake for 10–15 minutes until the pastry is tinged golden brown (remember it will be dark in colour thanks to the teff flour).

Meanwhile, make the filling. Put the coconut flour in a large mixing bowl and use a balloon whisk to gradually stir in the cream, preventing lumps. Add the sugar and eggs, whisking until combined, then whisk in the lemon zest and juice.

Remove the tin from the oven and immediately pour the lemon cream mixture onto the hot pastry. Return to the oven and bake for 30 minutes, turning halfway through cooking, until the topping is set.

Remove from the oven and leave to cool completely in the tin. Once the cake has cooled, use the foil to lift the whole thing out onto a board. Sprinkle with extra caster sugar (not icing sugar, as that will dissolve) and cut into bars.

COOK'S NOTES

❊ The pastry quantity given here makes enough for 2 trays of bars and a few cookies. Alternatively, halve the recipe, which leaves you with half a beaten egg. Wrap the excess pastry in baking parchment and freeze in a freezer bag for another time.

❊ You can happily swap the teff for many other gluten-free flours; it depends on availability and taste. I particularly like chestnut with the lemon topping. However, don't try to use coconut flour in this pastry – it's a different beast and requires a different ratio of liquid ingredients.

❊ I often make ground almonds from scratch as they have a much better flavour. See page 140 for the method and bear in mind that you will need to start with 230–250g/7½–8oz whole almonds to produce 200g/7oz ground meal; the skinning and roasting process typically results in a loss of 17 per cent.

❊ The excess pastry makes decent gluten-free shortbread-style cookies, but do add some chunky flavourings. I've found a mixture of dried fruit and walnuts the most successful.

❊ You don't have to roll the pastry, nor do you need to relax it: just slice it thinly and press it evenly into the baking tray.

❊ Not happy with the quantity of cream here? David Lebovitz's whole lemon bars topping is a good alternative. To do it, cut 1 whole unwaxed lemon (or 2 limes) into chunks, remove the seeds and process in a blender until smooth. Add 200g/7oz caster sugar, 3 tbsp extra lemon or lime juice, 3 large eggs, 4 tsp cornflour, ¼ tsp salt and 3 tbsp melted butter, and blend again until smooth. Proceed as above, but reduce the oven temperature to 150°C/300°F/Gas 2 when you pour the fruit mixture over the pastry and bake for 25 minutes until the topping is barely set.

ALMOND CAKE

The secret of any really good wheat-free cake is not a catalogue of flour mixes, powders and sweeteners, but an ingredient with which all fine bakers are familiar: ground nuts. These keep the mixture moist after cooking. Whisked egg whites are important too, to keep the cake light.

SERVES 8–10

125g/4oz caster sugar
125g/4oz butter, softened,
    plus extra for greasing
3 large eggs, separated
150g/5oz barley flour
2 tsp baking powder
125g/4oz ground almonds
1 tsp grated orange zest
⅛ tsp ground cinnamon
sifted icing or powdered sugar,
    for dusting

Grease a 23cm/9in spring-clip cake tin with butter. Line the base with a circle of baking parchment, then grease the paper as well. Heat the oven to 180°C/350°F/Gas 4.

Meanwhile, measure out the sugar and set 5 tbsp of it aside to use in the meringue. Place the rest in a large mixing bowl with the butter and beat until pale and creamy. Beat in the egg yolks, then stir in the barley flour, baking powder, ground almonds, orange zest and cinnamon until well combined – the mixture will be quite stiff.

In a separate large bowl, whisk the egg whites until soft peaks form when the whisk is lifted from the foam. Gradually whisk in the reserved 5 tbsp sugar to give a stiff meringue.

Fold the meringue into the cake mixture to give a light batter. Tip it into the prepared cake tin and smooth over the surface. Bake for 25–30 minutes or until a skewer inserted in the centre of the cake comes out dry.

Remove the cake from the oven and leave to cool in the tin for 10 minutes before transferring it to a wire rack to cool further. Peel off the baking parchment and dust the cake with icing sugar before serving warm or cold.

COOK'S NOTES

❊ You can flavour the basic cream cheese frosting recipe (see page 163) with orange zest, juice and cinnamon to use as a frosting for this cake.
❊ If you prefer to split the cake and fill the centre with cream, jam or frosting, cook it in a spring-clip tin that is 20cm/8in in diameter.
❊ Swapping the barley flour for buckwheat flour and the orange zest for lemon will give a traditional Italian mountain region version of this cake, which would then be filled with blackcurrant jam and cream, as described in Anna del Conte's *The Classic Food of Northern Italy*.
❊ Fine cornmeal also suits this recipe and can be successfully matched with lime, lemon or orange, skipping the cinnamon if preferred.
❊ Millet flour results in a lovely pale cake with a tender crumb. In this case, skip the cinnamon, use lemon or lime zest and frost the cake with a combination of cream or cream cheese frosting, sweetened with elderflower cordial to taste.
❊ For the best result, grind the nuts yourself rather than buying packs of ready-ground almonds. Blanch unskinned almonds in boiling water for 30 seconds and drain. When they are cool enough to handle, squeeze the kernels from the skins. Heat the oven to 180°C/350°F/Gas 4, spread the nuts out on a baking tray and cook for 10 minutes. Leave to cool, then grind in a processor until fine.
❊ If making muffins, bake for about 20 minutes.

CHOCOLATE SPELT CAKE

Chocolate and fibre are probably two words that should never be used in the same sentence, although this heady cake is rich in both. A dense, moist, fudgey style of cake is the best choice for wholemeal wheat-type flours. Succulent prunes are a terrific substitute for high levels of butter in baking, and this recipe is consequently rather low in fat, if high in sugar.

SERVES 12

125g/4oz ready-to-eat stoned prunes

100ml/3½fl oz brandy

125g/4oz butter, diced

150g/5oz dark chocolate, roughly chopped

500g/1lb caster sugar

340g/11½fl oz wholemeal spelt flour,
    or other wheat-type flour

2 tsp baking powder

75g/3oz cocoa powder

2 eggs, beaten

250g/8oz walnuts, roughly chopped

sifted icing or powdered sugar, or cocoa powder,
    to decorate

Bring a kettle of water to the boil. Grease a 23cm/9in square cake tin and line it with baking parchment.

Roughly chop the prunes and place in a food processor (a small one if you have it) with 2 tbsp hot water from the kettle. Purée until smooth. Transfer the purée to a large, heatproof mixing bowl.

Add the brandy, butter, chocolate and sugar to the mixing bowl. Pour in 250ml/8fl oz hot water from the kettle. In a large saucepan, place the remaining water from the kettle and bring it to simmering point.

Set the bowl over the saucepan, ensuring that the base of the bowl does not touch the top of the water, and leave the mixture to melt together gently, stirring occasionally until thick and smooth. Remove the bowl from the top of the saucepan and set aside to cool until lukewarm. Meanwhile, heat the oven to 160°C/325°F/Gas 3.

Sift the flour, baking powder and cocoa into a large mixing bowl. Make a well in the centre and pour in the chocolate mixture. Stir to gradually incorporate the dry ingredients from the side of the bowl into the wet. Beat in the eggs to give a smooth batter, then stir in the chopped nuts.

Transfer the mixture to the prepared tin, smooth over the surface and bake for 60–75 minutes or until a skewer inserted in the centre of the cake comes out clean. Remove the cake from the oven and leave to stand in the tin for 15 minutes before turning it out on to a rack to cool completely. Dust with sifted icing sugar or cocoa powder before serving.

COOK'S NOTES

✳ I tend to keep Lindt Excellence 70% in the kitchen for cooking because it's readily available and reasonably priced compared to many fine dark chocolates. If you use a different brand of chocolate, the result could be quite different but not necessarily in a negative way.

✳ Dried apricots used instead of prunes and amaretto in place of brandy give a sensational result (maybe the best). You can also use rum or port in this mixture.

✳ The flavour of the cake improves on keeping.

OATMEAL AND PECAN CAKE

Oats are especially associated with Celtic cooking and, almost by definition, are an austere style of food: think oatcakes and brose. Americans, however, have a different attitude. Although they consume oatmeal as porridge and define it as nourishing, they also use it in the most comforting home baking such as cakes, cookies and muffins. Matching oatmeal with luxurious pecans, coconut and a rich toffee topping, as in this recipe, is typical of the standpoint, and makes use of their native nut, the pecan.

SERVES 12

100g/3½oz medium oatmeal
150ml/¼ pint hot water
125g/4oz plain wheat flour
100g/3½oz caster sugar
100g/3½oz brown sugar
½ tsp bicarbonate of soda
½ tsp salt
¼ tsp ground cinnamon
⅛ tsp grated or ground nutmeg
175g/6oz unsalted butter, softened, plus extra for greasing
1 tsp vanilla extract
1 egg

For the topping

3 tbsp roughly chopped pecans or walnuts
40g/1½oz dried flaked coconut
half quantity of toffee sauce (see page 163)

Place the oatmeal in a medium bowl and cover with the measured hot water. Stir until smooth, then set aside to swell for 20 minutes. Meanwhile, in a mixing bowl, combine the flour, white and brown sugars, bicarbonate of soda, salt, cinnamon and nutmeg. Set aside.

Heat the oven to 180°C/350°F/Gas 4. Grease a loaf tin and line it with baking parchment.

In a large mixing bowl, beat the butter and vanilla extract together until soft and creamy. Beat in the egg, then add the thick oatmeal mixture a spoonful at a time, beating well after each addition.

Using a spatula, quickly fold in the flour mixture until fully incorporated. Transfer the batter to the prepared tin and smooth over the surface, allowing it to dip slightly along the middle to give a more even rise. Bake for 1 hour or until golden and firm. Remove from the oven and set aside to cool in the tin.

Meanwhile, make the topping. In a small saucepan, toast the chopped nuts until fragrant, then transfer to a heatproof mixing bowl to cool. Break up any very large flakes of coconut and add to the nuts. Make the toffee sauce according to the instructions on page 163 and stir it into the bowl of nuts.

Spread the topping over the cake while still in the tin and leave to set. When completely cold, carefully remove the cake from the tin and serve.

COOK'S NOTES

- The pecan, coconut and toffee topping is optional. If plain 'breakfast' or 'coffee' cakes are your thing, this basic cake recipe (which is not very sweet) is a good one to make. The batter can also be baked in muffin pans.
- Use a wholemeal wheat-type flour such as spelt in place of the white flour if desired, but flakes of barley and rye tend not to be as good as oatmeal. You could also use rolled oats.

WHEATBERRY AND HONEY CAKE

If you like solid, comforting fruit-and-vegetable-based cakes, you will probably love this one. The unpolished wheatberries add a hearty texture but some also seem to disappear mysteriously into the cake batter, so that the texture is not as sturdy as a cupful of grain may suggest. This recipe is based on one found in South Africa. The flavour is a little reminiscent of Britain's treacle tart, with only a hint of ginger. If you love this spice, use more.

SERVES 12

50g/2oz semi-pearled
   wheatberries
100g/3½oz butter, softened, plus extra
   for greasing
100g/3½oz brown sugar
1 egg, beaten
300g/10oz plain wheat flour
2 tsp baking powder
½ tsp ground ginger
125ml/4fl oz honey
125ml/4fl oz milk
½ tsp salt

Place the wheatberries in a small saucepan. Cover generously with water and bring to the boil. Reduce the heat and simmer until just tender – the exact time will depend on the variety and degree of pearling.

When cooked, drain and rinse the wheatberries, then measure them: you should have about 125ml/½ cup. Set aside to cool.

Meanwhile, grease a loaf tin well with butter and line it with baking parchment or foil, leaving some excess hanging over each side to help you lift the cake out later. Then grease the lining paper or foil as well.

Heat the oven to 180°C/350°F/Gas 4. In a large mixing bowl, beat the butter and sugar together until creamy and light. Gradually beat in the egg, then about half the flour, plus the baking powder and ginger. Beat in the honey, then gradually add the milk and the remaining flour, alternating between them.

Fold in the cooked wheatberries and transfer the cake batter to the prepared tin. Smooth over the surface, then make a furrow down the centre of the batter to encourage even rising. Bake for 1–1¼ hours or until a skewer inserted in the centre of the cake comes out clean.

Remove the cake from the oven and leave to stand in the tin for at least 10 minutes before lifting it out to cool further on a wire rack. Serve warm or cold.

COOK'S NOTES

✽ Wild rice can be used in place of the wheatberries, if you prefer, or just replace a portion of the wheat with wild rice. Any grains that find their way into the crust of the cake will become hard and crunchy.

✽ Mixing in 2 medium overripe bananas, about 250g/8oz mashed, gives a lovely banana cake that is delicious with wild rice. If you want to retain a spicy flavour, you need to bump up the ginger and/or add some more spices to compensate for the strong taste of the fruit.

✽ You can use golden syrup or treacle instead of the honey if preferred.

TORTA SBRISOLONA

A gorgeous cornmeal and almond shortbread, traditionally smashed in the centre to be devoured in crumbling chunks with sticky wines or grappa. Do not skimp on the quantity of vanilla – it is important to the flavour. Also, be sure never to use vanilla essence or 'flavouring'. They are cheap because they are substantially inferior to pure vanilla extract, for which there are regulations governing production. The intoxicating aroma and rich taste of vanilla are, as Alan Davidson's *The Oxford Companion to Food* states, 'unreproducible in the laboratory'.

SERVES 8–12

- 300g/10oz plain wheat flour
- 100g/3½oz coarse yellow cornmeal
- 100g/3½oz fine yellow cornmeal
- 150g/5oz almonds, chopped
- 200g/7oz caster sugar
- finely grated zest of 1 lemon
- 225g/7½oz butter, cubed, plus extra for greasing
- 3 eggs
- 1 tbsp vanilla extract
- sifted icing or powdered sugar, for dusting

Heat the oven to 180°C/350°F/Gas 4 and grease two 23cm/9in round or square cake tins. In a large mixing bowl, combine the plain wheat flour, the 2 cornmeals, plus the almonds, sugar and lemon zest. Use your fingertips to rub the butter into the dry ingredients until the mixture resembles breadcrumbs.

In a small bowl, beat the eggs and vanilla extract together. Make a well in the centre of the flour mixture and pour in the eggs. Give it a brief stir, then quickly finish working the dry ingredients into the wet using your hands to give a solid, pastry-like dough. Do not knead the dough; work it until it only just comes together.

Press the dough into the prepared tins. Smooth the surface over but leave it dimpled, as this will enhance the crumbly texture. Bake for 35–40 minutes until the top is just starting to brown. Leave the cakes to cool in the tins. Dust with sifted icing sugar and break into chunks to serve.

COOK'S NOTES

- Hazelnuts are sometimes used in place of, or in conjunction with, almonds.
- For extra shortness, replace half the butter with the same quantity of lard.
- Some Italian cooks believe that only finely ground cornmeal should be used in this cake.
- Some people prefer a softer, cakier style than the recipe here, but I think it important that the torta is not too thick – about 2.5–3cm/ 1–1¼in deep in the tins is best. If it's any thicker, the result will be too scone-like. Shape any excess into walnut-sized balls and bake as cookies, which my husband loves. Or shape the whole mixture into cookies! They will need only 20 minutes in the oven.

CRUNCHY OAT AND COCONUT SLICE

In Britain, these are called flapjacks, a term very confusing to the rest of the English-speaking world because they quite clearly don't flap. At my first job in London, I drove the man with the sandwich trolley crazy for 18 months because I was unable to grasp the concept of a thick, stiff, resolutely unflappable flapjack. Seeing that they were made from oats, I made matters worse by calling them oatcakes. This melt-and-mix recipe is terrific for children, which I say with some authority because it was one of the first things I ever made.

SERVES 12

225g/7½oz butter
250g/8oz rolled oats
160g/5½oz brown sugar
100g/3½oz desiccated coconut

Heat the oven to 160°C/325°F/Gas 3. In a large saucepan, slowly melt the butter over a gentle heat. Using a wooden spoon, stir in the oats, sugar and coconut, mixing until well combined.

Transfer the mixture to a 20cm/8in square tin and press it out evenly. Bake for 20–25 minutes or until light golden. Leave to cool in the tin, then cut into pieces and serve.

COOK'S NOTES

❋ To make fruited versions of this slice, simply stir in about 75g/3oz sultanas or raisins, chopped dried apricots, prunes, mango or other dried fruit at the same time as adding the oats, sugar and the coconut.
❋ Walnuts are a terrific addition, but other nuts will also work well. Add about 60g/2¼oz (chopped) to this quantity of mixture.
❋ Warm spices such as cinnamon, nutmeg and ginger can also be added. Use 1–1½ tsp in total of your favourites and add them along with the dry ingredients.
❋ Don't use coarsely shredded coconut or coconut flakes. It might seem as though they will look more attractive, but they make the mixture less absorbent than desiccated coconut, so the baked result is greasy and uncohesive.
❋ If the corners of the slice are browning too quickly, cover them with some foil.

BELLIES

Uncooked amaranth adds a wonderful crunchy texture to these traditional Mexican cornmeal cookies, which really appeal to children and adults, whether health food fans or not. Sunshine-yellow masa harina, in which the grain has been alkali treated, is a beautifully fine and light flour that can be used in all sorts of baking and gives a vibrant colour to the finished dish. Why these are called bellies I don't know. You'll certainly get one if you eat too many, but it might be a reference to the dried fruit, which could be said to resemble a navel.

MAKES 24

150g/5oz butter, softened, plus extra
    for greasing
160g/5½oz caster sugar
3 eggs, beaten, plus 1 egg yolk,
    beaten, to glaze
300g/10oz masa harina
1 tsp baking powder
250g/8oz amaranth
4 tbsp raisins or sultanas

Heat the oven to 180°C/350°F/Gas 4 and lightly grease a large baking sheet.

In a large mixing bowl, beat the butter and sugar together until light and fluffy. Beat in the whole eggs, then quickly start to beat in the masa harina and baking powder. Once a dough has been formed, add the amaranth and mix well.

Grease your hands with a little butter. Shape the mixture into balls about the size of a walnut and press a raisin or sultana into the centre of each. Set them well apart on the baking sheet and glaze with the beaten egg yolk. Place in the oven to bake for 20 minutes or until golden brown.

Remove from the oven and transfer to a wire rack to cool. Store in an airtight container.

COOK'S NOTES

✳ It is possible to use regular yellow or white cornmeal in this recipe, but choose a fine grind, as there is already enough grittiness in the mixture thanks to the amaranth.

✳ Sorghum flour is a great alternative to cornmeal here, and the amaranth can be swapped for teff grains.

✳ For a delicious wholegrain version of thumbprint cookies, skip the dried fruit and press the handle of a wooden spoon into the centre of each ball of cookie dough to make a hollow. Place them on the baking tray and fill the hollows three-quarters full with jam or (even better) lemon curd before baking as given.

✳ Cornmeal cookies are also traditional in countries such as France and Italy. For Italian biscotti to serve with coffee, rub together 150g/5oz stoneground cornmeal, 50g/2oz plain wheat flour, 100g/3½oz butter and 1 tsp lemon or orange zest until the mixture resembles breadcrumbs. Beat 1 large egg with 100g/3½oz sugar and 1 tsp vanilla extract, and stir this mixture into the dry ingredients to give a sticky dough. Shape into balls, space them well apart on a greased baking sheet and bake at 190°C/375°F/Gas 5 for 15 minutes or until the edges of the cookies start to brown.

ALEGRIA

This snack is well rooted in the traditional cooking of Central and South America. 'Alegria' in Spanish means happiness, and many travellers to Mexico will have encountered this popped amaranth sweet, although this one is based on a recipe from the Palenqueno people of Colombia.

MAKES 16

25g/1oz popped amaranth
(see Cook's Notes)
4 tbsp desiccated coconut
1–1½ tsp aniseed
7–8 tbsp runny honey

Place the amaranth, coconut and aniseed in a large mixing bowl and stir to combine evenly. Gradually and gently, stir in the honey to give a stiff but still bubbly dough without crushing the grains.

Have ready a double thickness of greaseproof paper. The mixture will be sticky. Using 2 dessert spoons, shape the grain mixture into balls about 2cm/¾in in diameter and place them on the paper, keeping them well spaced.

Leave to dry for several hours. During this time they will firm up on top, although little pools of honey will form at the base. Periodically, roll the balls over half a turn so that they are not wallowing in the syrup. Scoop up any clumps of mixture that stick to the paper and simply press the balls back into shape with your fingertips, then put them back to continue drying. The sweets will not become hard; they are ready when firm enough to pick up and eat using the fingers.

COOK'S NOTES

❖ Popping amaranth at home is easy to do but not easy to do well. You need to pop the grain in batches of only 1 tbsp at a time, making any substantial quantity tiresome to produce. Furthermore, many of the grains will burn before they pop and separating them from the others is a pain. Do yourself a favour and buy it industrially blasted with hot air by a proper factory.

❖ If you prefer to ignore this advice, use a frying pan or sauté pan (the amaranth doesn't jump very high) and have a bowl ready by the stove to hold the popped grains. Get the pan solidly hot, then add 1 tbsp amaranth and stir constantly with a thick, natural, bristled pastry brush. When most of the amaranth has popped, quickly tip it into the bowl, then add another tbsp of grain and repeat. You will have to do this 8 times to pop just 15g/½oz of grain, and some burning is inevitable.

❖ Other grains, including wild rice and millet, can be popped. Millet pops best in oil rather than a dry pan, but as it is such a small grain, the problem is how to fish it out of the hot oil once popped – you need a very fine-meshed, long-handled scoop of some kind. Also key is to ensure that the grain is covered by the oil, unlike popcorn that just sits on top of it. If there is not enough oil to cover the seeds, they will burn and the effect on the pan will be scary.

❖ Wild rice doesn't so much pop as poufs, swelling up like a crusty pillow. It tastes very nice, especially salted but, again, be sure that the grains are covered by the oil and, before deciding to make it, consider how you are going to scoop the finished grains from the oil.

ANZAC BISCUITS

During the First World War, it quickly became common usage to refer to the soldiers of the Australian and New Zealand Army Corps by its acronym. The first Anzac Day, which remains an annual remembrance event Down Under, was inaugurated on 25 April 1916 to commemorate the first anniversary of the landing of the Anzac troops at Gallipoli. These biscuits, devised by the women at home to send to the fighting men, had to be able to survive at least 2 months at sea on merchant navy ships, so are chewy and made without eggs.

MAKES 15–20

85g/3¼oz rolled oats
150g/5oz plain wheat flour
100g/3½oz sugar
50g/2oz desiccated coconut
100g/3½oz butter, plus extra for greasing
1 tbsp golden syrup
½ tsp bicarbonate of soda
1 tbsp boiling water

Heat the oven to 150°C/300°F/Gas 2 and lightly grease a baking sheet. Place the oats, flour, sugar and coconut in a mixing bowl.

In a small saucepan, melt the butter and golden syrup together over a low heat. Meanwhile, place the bicarbonate of soda in a small bowl and pour on the boiling water. When the butter has melted, stir the soda solution into the saucepan so that the mixture foams up.

Pour the bubbly butter mixture into the bowl of dry ingredients and mix well to give a chunky dough. Place heaped teaspoonfuls of the mixture on the greased baking sheet, spacing them well apart.

Bake the Anzacs for 20 minutes, then remove them from the oven. Using a palette knife or fish slice, transfer the biscuits while still warm to a wire rack to cool before eating. Store in an airtight tin.

COOK'S NOTES

❊ Myriad recipes now exist for Anzacs, and they are sold mass-produced in Australian and New Zealand supermarkets with various flavourings, including macadamia nuts and wattleseeds. As with all traditional regional foods, every cook has a favourite recipe and tut-tuts at any version deemed to be inauthentic. I purse my lips and frown disapprovingly at Anzacs with a cakey texture. They are supposed to be chewy but softish.

❊ There is some dispute about whether coconut was an original ingredient – apparently it was not easy to buy in Australia during the First World War, or so some people claim – but it quickly came to be seen as one of the Anzac's characteristic ingredients. The other essentials are rolled oats, golden syrup (the binding agent), butter and bicarbonate of soda.

GRAHAM CRACKERS

Sylvester Graham was an early 19th-century champion of wholegrains and believed refined, industrially milled flour to be the root of social problems. He was ridiculed during his lifetime for his extreme views and temperance, but today we can look back and see that, while he might not have been able to prove why he was right about the nutritional benefits of wholegrains, he was clearly on the right track. Today, Graham crackers are largely associated with unhealthy treats, but even when eaten plain they have a lovely spiced flavour.

MAKES 24

200g/7oz plain wheat-type flour
150g/5oz wholemeal wheat flour
200g/7oz rye flour
1½ tsp baking powder
¾ tsp ground cinnamon
½ tsp grated or ground nutmeg
½ tsp salt
75g/3oz unsalted butter, softened
100g/3½oz light brown sugar
1 large egg, plus 1 yolk
120ml/4fl oz honey
1½ tbsp molasses

Heat the oven to 180°C/350°F/Gas 4. Sift the 2 wheat flours, rye flour, baking powder, cinnamon, nutmeg and salt together and set aside.

In the bowl of an electric mixer, beat the butter and sugar together until light and fluffy. Add the whole egg and yolk and beat until well combined, then mix in the honey and molasses. Gradually add the sifted dry ingredients, mixing well.

Line the bases of two 30 x 23cm/12 x 9in Swiss roll tins with baking parchment. Halve the dough and roll each piece out to a rectangle large enough to line the base of each tin.

Use the rolling pin to help you lift the dough into the tins, then use a knife to trim off any excess. Score each tray into 12 equal crackers and decorate by pricking them with the tines of a fork.

Bake for 9 minutes until the dough is only just firm. Remove from the oven and allow the crackers to cool before lifting them from the tins. Store in an airtight container.

COOK'S NOTES

✻ Graham crackers are the base of the classic American cheesecake crust. You can whizz up the cooked crackers in a processor with butter to make a crumb crust, or simply roll out the dough and use it to line the base and sides of a spring-clip tin. Bake blind at 180°C/350°F/Gas 4 for 8–10 minutes, then cool and fill with the cheesecake filling (see page 163) before baking again. Rolling the dough gives a charming, rustic look to the finished cheesecake.

✻ To make s'mores, spread half the crackers with chocolate praline paste, then top with marshmallows and grill for 1–2 minutes. Cover with the remaining crackers to make sandwiches.

RYE AND CHEESE CRACKERS

Cheese-flavoured crackers are a delight, though many people don't realize that they are best not served with fine cheeses – their flavour detracts too much from those that the artisan maker will have tried so hard to put into the cheese itself. But for nibbles with drinks and general snacking, cheese crackers are most welcome. This recipe is based on one from my friend Lorna Wing's first book on party food. The rye adds an East and Central European quality that makes this a good match for rich creamy pâtés, hams and mild cured sausages.

MAKES 20

125g/4oz rye flour, plus extra
    for dusting
100g/3½oz butter, finely diced, plus extra
    for greasing
100g/3½oz grated mature Cheddar
    cheese
½ tsp cayenne pepper
2 tbsp poppy seeds

In a large mixing bowl, rub the flour and butter together until they resemble fine breadcrumbs. Mix in the cheese, cayenne pepper and poppy seeds, and knead lightly together in the bowl to form a dough. Wrap in clingfilm and chill for at least 30 minutes.

Grease a large baking sheet lightly and set aside. Dust a work surface with flour and roll out the chilled dough until about 4mm/¼in thick. Use a cutter to shape the dough into rounds, then use a palette knife or fish slice to transfer them to the baking sheet. Re-roll the trimmings, cut them into rounds and add to the baking sheet. Cover and place in the fridge for 30 minutes.

Heat the oven to 190°C/375°F/Gas 5. Place the crackers in the oven and bake for 8–10 minutes or until their naturally greyish colour is beginning to turn a golden brown.

Remove from the oven and transfer to a wire rack to cool. Store in an airtight container.

COOK'S NOTES

❊ You can replace the poppy seeds with chia or sesame seeds, or with some very finely chopped walnuts if you prefer.
❊ Any stoneground wholemeal wheat-type flour can be used in place of the rye flour. You could also use plain wheat flour, or the same quantity of beremeal or other barley flour.
❊ Mustard powder or ground black pepper can be used instead of cayenne, and you may wish to increase the quantity of both to give a spicier biscuit. A small amount of celery seed is another delicious possibility here.
❊ Cheddar is not essential. Use any hard and strongly flavoured cheese in its place, such as Gruyère, Comté or pecorino.

OATCAKES

As Nigella Lawson says in *How to be a Domestic Goddess*, there is something very satisfying about making 'good plain fare such as oatcakes – as if you're doing something sober and basic and not entertaining yourself with fripperies'. Yet in many households where oatcakes are not the daily bread, as they once were in Scotland and Ireland, they have found their métier on the cheeseboard, the serving of which often indicates a proper dinner party. How chic it is to serve homemade crackers rather than shop-bought ones on these occasions.

MAKES 12

50g/2oz coarse oatmeal
50g/2oz medium oatmeal
50g/2oz beremeal or barley flour, plus extra for dusting
½ tsp salt
25g/1oz butter, plus extra for greasing
a little boiling water to mix

Heat the oven to 150°C/300°F/Gas 2 and lightly grease a baking sheet.

In a large mixing bowl, combine the oatmeals, beremeal and salt. Using a round-bladed knife, cut the butter into the mixture and stir to help distribute it. Make a well in the centre and pour in 1 tbsp or so of boiling water. Mix to give a stiff dough, adding more hot water if necessary.

Dust a work surface with the beremeal and roll out the dough into a thin square. Leave to rest for a few minutes, then cut the dough into squares or whatever your desired shape, trimming away any very craggy edges, but leaving the rims of the oatcakes rugged as the grains break away.

Using a palette knife or fish slice, transfer the oatcakes to the baking sheet and bake for about 30 minutes until only just beginning to brown. Remove from the oven and leave to cool. Store in an airtight tin.

COOK'S NOTES

- This recipe is based on one by Catherine Brown. The chunks of oats and beremeal give a pleasingly rugged texture, but you can make a smoother oatcake if you prefer, by using only medium or fine oatmeal.
- The beremeal can be replaced with the same quantity of fine oatmeal, or with wholemeal wheat or rye flour if desired.
- Melted dripping or bacon fat would often be used in place of butter. A mixture of lard and butter could also be used.
- Cut the oatcakes into rounds if you prefer, but the square shape offers an element of mild surprise that is welcome at dinner parties. It also stops you pfaffing around with dough trimmings.
- Oatcakes can also be baked on a griddle, or girdle or in a heavy frying pan. They need to cook slowly and steadily for a good 5 minutes so that they dry out thoroughly. The pan needs to be solidly hot, but not fiercely so.

POPCORN

From the foreigner's perspective, it can seem as though there is nothing that Americans won't do with popcorn, or Jell-O for that matter. Some recipes take a little getting used to (a popcorn version of bread and butter pudding springs to mind), especially as popcorn's texture is so naturally dry and crackly. Still, who of us doesn't associate a box of popcorn with a trip to the cinema? Homemade and flavoured popcorn can be a terrific indulgence and tremendous fun. Whether or not you make it low-fat and healthy is up to you.

SERVES 2–3

2 tbsp vegetable oil
about 50g/2oz popcorn

Place the oil in a large, heavy pot over a moderate heat.

Pour in enough popcorn to cover the base of the pot in a single layer, then cover and leave to cook so that the popcorn pops, shaking the pot occasionally.

When the popping noises become infrequent, remove the pot from the heat and serve, adding flavourings as desired.

Alternatively, use an air-popping machine according to the manufacturer's instructions.

COOK'S NOTES

✳ My favourite is to melt 25g/1oz butter with 2 tbsp crunchy peanut butter and stir it into the popcorn.
✳ Alternatively, mix with 4 tbsp grated Parmesan, 1 tsp chopped fresh oregano, ¼ tsp dried red chilli flakes and loads of salt and pepper.
✳ You could pop the corn in chilli oil, then sprinkle with 2 tbsp salt, 1 tbsp ground cumin, plus dried red chilli flakes and freshly ground pepper.
✳ For spicy fruit and nut popcorn, heat 4 tbsp oil in a wok. Add 175g/6oz stoned Medjool dates and 85g/3¼oz dried apricots, both roughly chopped, plus 250g/8oz mixed nuts such as almonds, cashews and macadamias. Stir-fry until lightly browned, then mix in the popped corn and turn until the ingredients stick together a little. Turn off the heat. Stir in the grated zest of 1 lemon or lime, a finely chopped chilli, 2 tbsp coriander leaves, 1 tbsp torn basil, plus salt and pepper.
✳ To make popcorn balls, melt 3 tbsp butter in a large saucepan. Add 200g/7oz marshmallows, chopped, and 3 tbsp brown sugar and stir until melted. Remove from the heat and mix in the popped corn and 125g/4oz M&Ms or Smarties. Butter your hands, shape the mixture into balls and place on baking parchment to dry.
✳ Make popcorn and peanut brittle by stirring the popped corn and 150g/5oz salted peanuts into hot toffee sauce (see page 163). Pack into an oiled and lined cake tin (oil the lining paper too) and bake for 20 minutes at 180°C/350°F/Gas 4. When done, spoon the mixture into a cold tin, also oiled and lined. Leave until set, then cut into pieces and serve.

MEALIE CANDY

Home candy making is something of a lost art, but fun to do occasionally, especially as it allows you to use tasty, wholesome flavourings such as toasted oatmeal that most sweets manufacturers wouldn't touch with a bargepole. The small investment in a candy or sugar thermometer will make this sweet even easier to make.

MAKES 25

50g/2oz coarse oatmeal
a little vegetable oil or butter, for greasing
500g/1lb caster sugar
300ml/½ pint water
4 tbsp treacle
1 tsp lemon juice
2 tbsp finely chopped glacé ginger
2 tbsp finely chopped walnuts

In a heavy saucepan, toast the oatmeal over a moderate heat, stirring constantly until the grains are browned and fragrant. Transfer to a bowl to cool and wipe out the pan.

Lightly grease a small cake tin. Line with foil, leaving some excess over the sides of the tin so that the candy is easy to remove later. Grease the foil lining and set the tin aside ready to pour the hot candy into it.

Combine the sugar, water, treacle and lemon juice in the saucepan. Place over a low heat until the sugar has dissolved, stirring occasionally, then bring the mixture to the boil. Boil vigorously without stirring for several minutes until the syrup reaches 115°C/240°F on a candy thermometer.

Immediately remove the pan from the heat and, with a wooden spoon or paddle, beat the syrup until it just starts to form a mass of little white specks but before it becomes very thick.

Working quickly, stir in the oatmeal, ginger and walnuts and pour the mixture into the prepared tin. Smooth over the surface and leave to cool. When the mixture has almost set, mark it into squares with a knife. To serve, lift the block of candy from the tin and break it up into pieces following the line of the cuts made earlier.

COOK'S NOTES

- The lemon juice adds some flavour but also plays an important role in preventing the early granulation of the sugar syrup. In its place you could use a pinch of cream of tartar.
- The specific temperature the sugar syrup needs to reach is also known as the 'soft ball stage'. It is possible to test for this without a candy thermometer, but it does make working swiftly enough more problematic. To test for soft ball stage, drop a little of the syrup into a glass of cold water and leave to cool for a few minutes. The syrup is at the right temperature when it can be picked out of the water and rolled into a soft ball between the fingers.
- Ginger and walnut are just 2 of the flavours that can be used in this type of candy. You may prefer other nuts or glacé fruit, or to add some coconut and orange zest. Maple syrup would also make a nice addition here.
- Preserved stem or crystallized ginger can be used in place of glacé ginger if necessary.

BASIC RECIPES

Combine these versatile recipes with the grain dishes featured in the book to make complete meals.

Shellfish butter

You will need 200g/7oz of seafood shells and heads per 60g/2½oz salted butter. If you are using prawn shells exclusively, you can blend them with the butter in a food processor until smooth and soft. If you are including crab shells or other hard seafood shells, pound them with the butter in a mortar until the mixture is as smooth as you can manage. Push through a sieve, then scrape the flavoured butter into a roll, wrap in foil and store in the freezer. Slice off portions as you need them.

Shellfish stock

Make a mirepoix using 50g/2oz each of chopped carrot, onion and celery. Melt 15g/1 tbsp butter in a pot and fry the mirepoix for 4 minutes or so. Add 350g/12oz whole shellfish (small crabs and/or prawns) and 3 tbsp Noilly Prat vermouth, sherry or brandy and fry for another couple of minutes. Add 1.2 litres/ 2 pints fish stock, 1 roughly chopped tomato and a sprig of tarragon. A pinch of cayenne and a bay leaf are optional. Simmer over a low heat for 40 minutes. Strain through a fine sieve, pressing down on the solids to extract as much flavour as possible.

Grilled chicken

Use chicken breast fillets for this. Lay each one in turn between two sheets of clingfilm on a work surface. Using a mallet or heavy rolling pin, bash along the chicken until it is evenly thin. Place in a non-corrosive container such as a Pyrex or ceramic dish and cover with 3–4 tbsp olive or vegetable oil, the juice of half a lemon (and/ or some soy sauce), a crushed garlic clove and some salt and pepper. Leave to marinate for at least an hour. To cook, heat a ridged grill pan over a very high heat until you can see the haze rising from the surface. Lift the chicken from the marinade, lay it on the pan and immediately reduce the heat to medium. Cook for 1 minute on each side – it doesn't take long because the fillets are so thin. Alternatively, cook under a hot overhead grill or salamander.

Grilled beefsteak

Lay your steaks in turn between 2 sheets of clingfilm on a work surface. Using a mallet or heavy rolling pin, bash the meat until it is evenly thin. Place in a non-corrosive container. Cover with 3–4 tbsp olive or vegetable oil, the same quantity of red wine (or just a splash of red wine vinegar; for Asian dishes use soy sauce), plus a crushed garlic clove and some salt and pepper. Add robust herbs such as thyme, sage or rosemary if you like. Leave to marinate for at least an hour. To cook, heat a ridged grill pan over a very high heat until you can see the haze rising from the surface. Lay the steak on the grill-pan and immediately lower the heat to medium. Cook for 1 minute, then turn and cook on the other side for another minute. The thinness of the bashed meat makes it cook quickly and therefore stay juicy. Alternatively, cook under a hot overhead grill or salamander.

Grilled prawns

You will probably want to serve around 3–5 large prawns per person. Choose raw or 'green' prawns – frozen if you like. Remove the heads, shells and tails if desired – you may only want to take off the heads and the legs under the belly. Place in a non-corrosive dish and cover with 6 tbsp olive or vegetable oil, a crushed garlic clove, some lemon juice or soy sauce, a little chopped chilli and some salt and pepper. Marinate for at least an hour – longer if the prawns are frozen and you are using the marinating period in tandem with defrosting. To cook, heat a ridged grill pan over a very high heat until you can see the haze rising from the surface. Lift the prawns from the marinade, letting the excess drip away. Lay them on the grill pan and immediately lower the heat to medium. Cook for 1½ minutes on each side. Alternatively, cook under a hot overhead grill or salamander.

Grilled fish

You can use whole fish or large fillets for this method. Clean and trim the fish as necessary. If the fish is whole, make a few diagonal slashes along each side with a sharp knife. Rub some olive or vegetable oil all over the fish and season lightly. Heat a grill pan over a very high heat until you can see the haze rising from the surface. Lay the fish on the pan and immediately lower the heat to medium. Cook for 3–5 minutes on each side depending on the size and meatiness of the individual species. Alternatively, cook under a hot overhead grill or salamander.

Pan-roast fish

Choose fillets of meaty fish such as sea bass, barramundi and salmon for this method. It also suits guinea fowl. Heat the oven to 200°C/400°F/ Gas 6. Brush an ovenproof frying pan lightly with oil. Place it over a high heat until you can see the haze rising from the surface. Lightly season the fish fillets and place them in the pan skin-side down. Using a fish slice, press down firmly on the fish to help sear the skin, and cook for 1–2 minutes. Transfer the frying pan to the hot oven and bake for 10 minutes. Alternatively, if you don't have an ovenproof pan, you can sear the fish on the oven top and transfer it to a greased baking tray before placing it in the oven.

Roast chicken

Heat the oven to 220°C/425°F/ Gas 7. Line a roasting tin with a double thickness of foil. Brush the chicken all over with olive oil, then massage it with 15g/½oz or so of butter, a crushed clove of garlic and some salt and pepper. Place the chicken in the roasting tin and add 125ml/4fl oz water. Roast for 15 minutes, then reduce the heat to 190°C/375°F/Gas 5 and roast for 25 minutes. Remove the roasting tray from the oven, leaving it on, and carefully turn the bird upside down to help it cook evenly and keep the breast meat moist. Baste it generously with the pan juices and return to the oven for a further 25 minutes. The chicken is cooked when the thighs, when pierced with a skewer, exude clear rather than bloody juices. Remove from the oven and leave to rest for 10 minutes before carving. Skim the fat from the roasting tin and use the remaining pan juices as a sauce.

Roast lamb

Heat the oven to 250°C/500°F/ Gas 10 or the highest setting. Rub a small to medium leg of lamb all over with sea salt and freshly ground pepper and place it in a roasting tin. Place in the oven for 1 hour. That's it. This method from Barbara Kafka, it must be said, is controversial. If you prefer, you can roast the lamb at 230°C/450°F/ Gas 8 for 20 minutes, then reduce the heat to 200°C/400°F/Gas 6 and continue cooking for a further hour or so. To calculate the timing for this method, weigh the lamb before roasting. It needs to cook for 15 minutes per 500g/1lb after that initial 20 minutes in the oven at the higher temperature. Other options include using a shoulder of lamb instead of a leg. You can also rub the meat all over with olive oil, strew it with crushed sprigs of thyme or rosemary and/or tuck some unpeeled garlic cloves around the meat. After cooking, and setting the lamb aside to rest for 15 minutes, make a sauce from the pan juices by first skimming off the fat from the roasting tin. Place the roasting tin over a high heat and pour in about 350ml/12fl oz lamb stock, plus a slug of red or white wine if desired. Stir the pan vigorously with a wooden spoon to scrape up and incorporate the caramelized cooking juices while bringing the liquid to a vigorous boil. Boil until the volume of liquid has reduced by half, add the juices the resting lamb has exuded and strain the sauce before serving.

Poached beef

Choose good-quality beef fillet steaks for this dish. Bring a generous quantity of beef or veal stock to the boil in a large saucepan.

Add a few vegetables or flavourings if desired, but no salt. Reduce the heat so that the stock only just simmers and lay the meat in the pan. Cook at this low temperature for 3–5 minutes, or a bit longer, depending on how well done you prefer your meat and its exact size. Be aware that a more vigorous boil will cause the meat to toughen. Lift the steaks from the stock and serve as desired. The broth can be served with the steaks if required, or used in sauces, soups, stews and so on.

Deep-fried chillies

Padrón peppers from north-western Spain are best for this (they are typically mild, though statistically 1 in 50 is very hot). Heat a heavy pan filled around 2.5cm/1in deep with olive oil. Add the whole chillies and fry for 2–3 minutes until just starting to brown. Lift the chillies from the oil and drain on a tray covered with several thicknesses of absorbent kitchen paper. Salt the chillies generously and serve.

Roast bell peppers or chillies

Heat the oven to 180°C/350°F/Gas 4. Rub the peppers or chillies with olive oil and place on a baking tray. Place in the oven for 15–20 minutes, or until just starting to brown and soften. Remove from the oven, leave to cool slightly and gently pull out the core and seeds before serving. If you want to roast the peppers or chillies so that they can be peeled, place them in the oven at 200°C/400°F/Gas 6 and roast for 20 minutes or until the skins are blackened and blistered. Remove from the oven, place in a bowl and cover the bowl with clingfilm. Leave to steam for 10–15 minutes. When cool enough to handle, peel the skins away and discard the core and seeds, but retain the cooking juices to add to your dish.

Wild mushroom sauce

Trim 125g/4oz fresh wild mushrooms as necessary and cut into large but even-sized pieces. In a large frying pan or sauté pan, heat 1 tbsp olive oil with 1 crushed garlic clove. Add the mushrooms and 1 tsp chopped parsley and cook for 3–5 minutes, stirring. When the mushrooms have released all their liquid and the liquid has evaporated, stir in ½ tbsp tomato paste, season the mixture to taste with salt and pepper and keep cooking for a further 5 minutes before serving or further use.

Indispensable tomato sauce

In a small saucepan, place 400g/13oz canned, chopped plum tomatoes in natural juice. Add 25g/1oz butter or olive oil and half a small peeled onion, unsliced. Place over a low heat and leave to cook very gently, stirring occasionally, and whenever you feel like it, squashing the tomatoes against the side of the pan to make the sauce smoother. The sauce should be thick after 20–30 minutes, but if not done to your liking, keep cooking. Remove the onion. Season to taste with salt and pepper and add whatever herbs you fancy before serving or further use. For quick and easy 'baked beans', heat a drained can of small white beans such as navy or cannellini in the finished sauce until piping hot.

Chicken jus

Only use very good-quality chicken stock for this. In a small heavy saucepan, bring 225ml/7½fl oz stock to the boil and boil it very hard until it has reduced in volume by at least half. You may wish to boil it down further. The result will be a very intense but glossy clear gravy to spoon over and around chicken dishes. You can also do this in a roasting tin after roasting a chicken, setting it aside to rest and spooning off the excess fat from the tin. In this case, while bringing it to the boil on the stovetop, stir the sauce vigorously with a wooden spoon to incorporate the caramelized cooking juices from the base of the tin. Add a slug of white wine, or some sherry or brandy, while it is boiling. Adjust the seasoning to taste before serving.

Korean chilli sauce

Finely chop 1 large garlic clove and 1½ spring onions. Combine them in a small bowl with 1½ tsp rice vinegar or cider vinegar, ½ tbsp sesame oil, 1 tsp sesame seeds, 1 tsp granulated or caster sugar and 1 tbsp kochujang (Korean red pepper paste). If the authentic Korean paste is unavailable, use Chinese red chilli paste.

Dashi

In a stockpot, place 2 litres/3½ pints water and a 10cm/4in

piece of kombu seaweed. Place over a moderate heat and cook for 10 minutes without letting it boil. When the kombu has fully expanded, add 30g/1¼oz dried bonito flakes (katsuo-bushi) and simmer gently for 5 minutes. Remove from the heat and leave the pot to stand until the fish flakes settle at the bottom. Strain the stock, discarding the solids, before further use. Reasonable instant dashi powder is available.

Coconut broth
Bring 450ml/¾ pint fish stock, or vegetable or chicken stock, and 6 tbsp dry white wine to the boil in a small saucepan. Boil hard until the liquid has reduced in volume by about half. Remove from the heat and stir in 150–175ml/¼ pint–6fl oz good-quality coconut cream. Return to a gentle heat and warm through. Adjust the seasoning to taste with salt and pepper, plus a hint of Thai fish sauce or soy sauce if desired, and serve warm with fish and seafood dishes.

Quick berry compote
Pick over and rinse several handfuls of mixed berries and place them in a heavy pan with 1 tbsp caster sugar. Stir, then cover and cook gently over a very low heat for 10–15 minutes, stirring frequently to prevent sticking.

Toffee sauce
Combine 400g/13oz sugar, ¼ tsp cream of tartar, a pinch of salt and 6 tbsp water in a large, heavy saucepan. Place over a low heat

and leave to cook, without stirring, for 2–5 minutes until some sugar begins to melt and turn golden. Raise the heat to medium and continue cooking, stirring occasionally, until all the sugar has melted and the caramel is a deep golden colour (or, more specifically, the 150°C/300°F 'hard crack' stage). Pour 4 tbsp double cream slowly down the side of the pan, stirring constantly to combine. Transfer the sauce to a heatproof bowl and use as required.

Cream cheese frosting
In a mixing bowl, beat together 60g/2¼oz diced cream cheese, 30g/1¼oz butter, 1 tsp vanilla extract and 1 tsp lemon or lime zest until the mixture is smooth and fluffy. Sift 175g/6oz icing sugar and then gradually beat it into the cream cheese mixture until the frosting is well combined, creamy and light. This will make enough to cover the top and sides of a 23cm/9in cake.

Best-ever cheesecake filling
This makes enough to fill a 20cm/8in crust. In a mixing bowl, beat 750g/1½lb diced cream cheese and 1 tsp vanilla extract until smooth and fluffy. Set aside. In the bowl of an electric mixer, whisk 4 eggs together until thick and light, then gradually beat in 200g/7oz caster sugar. Slowly add spoonfuls of the cream cheese mixture to the egg mixture, beating until smooth after each addition. Mix in 1 tbsp grated lemon zest and 2 tsp lemon juice. Pour the mixture

into the prepared crust and bake at 180°C/350°F/Gas 4 for 25–30 minutes. The most important bit: open the oven door and leave the cheesecake to cool right down in the oven. Only then place it in the fridge to chill.

Crumb crust
Place 225g/7½oz broken crackers or biscuits in a food processor and pulse to give fine crumbs. Add 5 tbsp caster sugar and some spices if desired, then, with the machine running, pour in 125g/4oz melted butter. Remove the dough from the processor and divide it into 2 or 3 pieces. Place a piece in the bottom of a spring-clip cake tin. Using the base of a large, heavy glass, press the dough out across the base of the tin to give a thin, firmly packed crust. Work the rest of the mixture up and around the side of the tin and fill in any gaps. Chill for 30 minutes before filling.

Rich sweet pastry
Sift 200g/7oz plain wheat flour into a mixing bowl and make a well in the centre. Dice 100g/3½oz butter and add to the bowl with an egg yolk, 2 tsp caster sugar, ½ tsp salt and 3 tbsp water. Using the fingertips of one hand, work the ingredients together until they form a dough – add a little more water if necessary. Knead lightly for 1–2 minutes, then shape into a ball, wrap in clingfilm and chill for at least 30 minutes before rolling out. This gives enough to line a 20cm/8in tart tin with some left over to form a pie top.

SUPERGRAINS DIRECTORY

WHEAT

EINKORN • EMMER • FARRO • FREEKEH • KAMUT • PETIT ÉPEAUTRE • SPELT • WHEATBERRIES

Wheat is
mild, sweet, chewy, crunchy, elastic, hearty, toasty

It goes with
chicken, nuts, mushrooms, dried fruit, cream, honey, dried ginger

It's good to eat for
calcium, copper, fibre, folate, iron, magnesium, manganese, phosphorus, protein, vitamins B1, B3 and E, zinc

Heard about the amazing ancient grain farro that's good for people who can't eat wheat? Farro is wheat. Are you buying loads of spelt bread and pasta these days because you can't eat wheat? Spelt is wheat. What about Kamut? That's wheat too. So is einkorn, emmer and petit épeautre. It is a great testament to the simple deliciousness and versatility of wheat that, even when people are trying to avoid it, they keep eating it.

Don't get me wrong, the wider availability of different wheat options is a good thing. I'm sceptical of the premiums charged for these trendy products. I usually have a bag of semi-perlato (semi-pearled) farro in the cupboard, often buy spelt bread and linguine and tend to use white spelt in place of plain or all-purpose flour. It's the fact that these alternative products are wheat that makes them so useful. They segue seamlessly into everyday meals. My husband and daughter have no idea they are eating spelt or farro, nor do they care. (It is a myth, by the way, that alternative wheats are all low in gluten: their gluten levels and structure vary.)

Few of us need to eat more refined or processed grain products, however, so while you're in the organic health food store take a look at simple cracked wheat – wholegrain wheatberries that are lightly milled into smaller pieces without harming the nutritious bran and germ layers. This traditional product offers all the health benefits of wholegrain wheatberries (folate, calcium, phosphorus, zinc, copper, iron, vitamin E and B vitamins) but with a much faster cooking time. Quick-cooking bulgur wheat can be used in similar ways to cracked wheat but is a more heavily processed product; for this, the wholewheat is part-cooked, then dried and broken into pieces.

Freekeh, another fashionable ancient grain food, is usually made from wheat but need not be. Young spears of green wheat or barley are roasted to give a rich, smoky and somewhat meaty taste – delicious. Freekeh is very high in usable protein and fibre, and provides a much greater degree of satiety than, say, white rice. It's a good source of calcium too. There is also anecdotal evidence to suggest that people intolerant to wheat can consume freekeh. In Germany, green spelt is roasted over beechwood fires to create an almost identical product that can be found in upmarket health food retailers in the UK.

RICE

CHINESE EMPEROR • FORBIDDEN BLACK RICE • VENERE NERO • BROWN • RED • GREEN • WHITE

Rice is
fragrant, tender, light, delicate, starchy, refreshing, absorbent

It goes with
meats, poultry, seafood, pulses, nuts, herbs, spices, milk

It's good to eat for
magnesium, manganese, phosphorus, selenium, vitamins B1, B3 and B6

There was a time when buying rice (*Oryza sativa*) was a simple choice of white or brown, and for most of us that meant white. They are essentially the same product: one stripped bare, leaving little to the imagination, the other puritanically still wearing its seed coat. But a bright new collection of colourfully coated rices is finding its way onto store shelves and research laboratories, and recent discoveries about their health benefits are making the old binary choice of white or brown rice redundant.

As we've seen with fresh fruits and greens, it seems the darker or more brightly coloured the rice grain, the more antioxidants it contains. Researchers at Cornell University found that black rice (and they studied 12 different varieties of black rice) had a greater content of health-promoting phenolics, flavonoids and anthocyanins than common brown or white rice. Black rice bran has also been found to be more effective than brown in protecting against inflammation.

Even if you can't find Chinese emperor or Forbidden black rice, or Piedmont's Venere nero or black Venus rice, on the shelves, the importance of choosing a wholegrain variety (brown, red or even green) is well established. Antioxidant-rich wholegrain rice is more effective than white in assisting weight loss and increasing good HDL cholesterol, better at inhibiting breast and colon cancer and better help in preventing and controlling diabetes.

Convinced? Then the important thing to know is that you shouldn't throw wholegrain rice into your next risotto or paella thinking it will just take a bit longer to cook. It will take For-Ev-Ver and taste terrible. The ingredients of the stock and any flavouring vegetables in the pan lower the overall boiling temperature. This means that while wholegrain rice might take 40 minutes to cook in plain boiling water, it can easily take 90 minutes in a risotto-style dish and still be a bit too chewy. The wholegrain rice's layer of bran also prevents absorption of the stock, so it may seem you need to add more, but this results in an over-seasoned, unpleasant mixture.

Being very plump and chewy, short-grain whole rices are best for salads and stews or braises cooked in the oven. Alternatively, boil them in plain water, then drain and toss them with sauce as is done with pasta, bearing in mind the colour will leach from brightly coloured rice and can taint your other ingredients. Boiling and tossing is the method of choice for long-grain whole rices too.

RYE

Rye is
plump, juicy, sweet, dark, chewy, heavy, fruity

It goes with
salmon, ham, cheese, caraway, nutmeg, molasses, cherries

It's good to eat for
calcium, copper, fibre, iron, magnesium, manganese, phosphorus, potassium, selenium, vitamins B3 and E, zinc

Growing up in body-conscious Australia in the 1970s, I feel like I've known forever that rye was good for you – all those ads for Ryvita, with the tape measure pulling round the unfeasibly slender waist. Is it even possible to eat a slice of pumpernickel and not know it's doing you good?

Fortunately, science has finally caught up and we have a certifiable superfood growing right under our noses, not in a remote location on the other side of the world. Rye promotes weight control. It suppresses hunger, improves digestive health and protects against colon cancer. Then there are the cardiovascular benefits, including reducing blood pressure and the risk of heart disease. It enhances insulin secretion and improves b-cell function, is high in iron, calcium, potassium and zinc, plus the vitamin E and the B group.

What's not to like? True, the whole grains take a long time to cook – over an hour – but their sweet juiciness is delicious and they make ideal nourishment for wintry weather. Even so, baked goods made from rye flour are the usual way to encounter this underrated grain.

Rye bread in myriad forms is the traditional favourite of northern and Eastern Europe. Germany's dark, dense pumpernickel, which blends rye crumbs or flour with sweet ingredients such as molasses, cinnamon and hazelnuts, was originally a way of minimizing wastage by using the coarsest grains. It has many relatives, often flavoured with molasses, but also cocoa, coffee, caramel and caraway. Rye is also made into light, aromatic breads and is particularly good if sourdough starter is used.

In her brilliant book, *The Food and Cooking of Eastern Europe*, Lesley Chamberlain explains why some people may struggle at first to get to grips with the distinctive flavour and texture of rye bread. 'A genuine rye loaf is not a "background" bread like a French stick, but one designed for the prominence of the hors-d'oeuvre or evening cold table, or for eating on its own, East European style, perhaps with yogurt or a glass of buttermilk.'

Cakes made from rye flour are traditional in the Netherlands. Rye flour is low in gluten, so do not expect baked goods made from it to rise substantially. Doughs will also be stickier than those made from wheat flours. This is not unappealing, just different. Whole cooked rye berries or flakes are a good addition to grainy breads, but for porridges and muesli they are best used with a light hand, in combination with other grains.

OATS

Oats are
unctuous, soft, rich, ambrosial, comforting, rugged, toasty

They go with
bacon, game, lamb, nuts, soft cheese, berries, muscovado sugar

It's good to eat for
calcium, copper, fibre, folate, iron, magnesium, manganese, phosphorus, protein, selenium, vitamins B1 and E, zinc

To appreciate the health benefits of oats requires little more than making a bowl of porridge. When you're done, add cold water to the dirty saucepan and let it soak. Soon the residual porridge will become a thick film and almost detach itself from the pan, leaving it virtually clean, as though the oats were a high-tech non-stick wonder product. You just know no bad cholesterol's going to stick to your arteries while that stuff's around.

Oats are a good source of protein (though not lysine), unsaturated fatty acids (including linoleic acid), iron, magnesium, B vitamins, calcium, folic acid and vitamin E, among other goodies. They help regulate blood sugar and reduce cravings for addictive substances, as well as strengthen the nerves. Oats are also believed to be an aphrodisiac for men – something that once had the monks of Ireland extremely concerned, so they made their gruel very watery. The phrase 'sowing your wild oats' pays tribute to this folk wisdom, but science has confirmed the theory. An oat extract, Exsativa, has been found in studies to prolong and intensify male sexual pleasure as well as increase the libido. So if you didn't think porridge was very sexy, perhaps you should think again.

You could find it more arousing if you made it with the good stuff: Scots or Irish steel-cut oats. These are whole kernels chopped into two or three pieces to give a very coarse meal that the Scots call pinhead. Truly anything else is a compromise. Rolled oats, which were developed in the USA, are pieces of pinhead oatmeal steamed to soften them and then rolled into flakes. Jumbo rolled oats are made by steaming and rolling the whole kernel. Both cook more quickly than proper pinhead oatmeal, but the heat of processing results in the loss of flavour and nutrients.

Instant oats are worse – you only need eat a bowl to figure that out – and in comparison to traditional oatmeal are highly refined. Dr Terry Shintani, of the University of Hawaii School of Medicine, is one nutrition expert who likens instant oats to refined white flour and sugar. Don't buy them.

It is, however, worth exploring the many savoury ways oats can be served. From Friesland's grünkohl, a hearty gammon, sausage and cabbage stew (see page 100), to creamy soups of France and the Czech Republic, and northern China's honeycomb oat noodles served with chilli dipping sauce, there really are a lot of sexy things you can do with oats besides make porridge.

BARLEY

PEARL BARLEY • POT BARLEY • BLACK BARLEY • BARLEY FREEKEH

Barley is

honeyed, luscious, pearly, fat, chewy, starchy, rugged

It goes with

lamb, duck, mushrooms, root vegetables, broccoli, oregano, apple, beer

It's good to eat for

calcium, copper, fibre, iron, magnesium, manganese, phosphorus, potassium, protein, selenium, vitamins B1, B3 and E, zinc

The cold, remote landscape of the Orkney Islands off the coast of the Scottish Highlands has little in common with the dramatic desert panorama of Tunisia (remember *Star Wars*?). The cuisines could not be more different. Compare the heavy breads and rib-sticking soups of one to the romantic, spicy sauces and light couscous dishes of the other. Yet both are home to barley.

Barley can grow almost anywhere, and was one of the first domesticated cereals. Why, then, do we often see it as a fringe Celtic curiosity? Elizabeth David, writing in *English Bread and Yeast Cookery* in 1977, said: 'Those who acquire a taste for it are likely to become addicts. I am one.' On that endorsement alone, the fact that barley bread isn't more common is perplexing.

Maybe Dr Nicholas Perricone can change that. He's put pot (also known as hulled) barley number three on his list of Top Ten Superfoods. It protects against cancer, keeps blood sugar levels stable, strengthens the cardiovascular system, promotes a healthy intestinal tract, and improves disease resistance.

While well-known traditional uses for barley such as Scotch broth may not be at the forefront of culinary trends, many of the popular dishes in today's global kitchen – risotto, couscous, freekeh – can be made with barley, and authentically so. I am

a particular fan of Orkney beremeal, a stoneground flour made from kiln-roasted local barley, and often use its smoky taste to give oomph to fruit crumble toppings.

Pearl barley is the most widely available form, though it is worth noting that – although it never says so on the packet – there are two types, one being more diligently polished and therefore whiter and starchier than the other. The white polished type (usually sold under Asian brands) is not 'wholegrain'; the tan-coloured type isn't whole either but does retain some of the important bran. Pot (hulled) barley is barley that's kept its fully-lined outdoor coat on, and consequently takes longer to soften.

You can expect to hear more about naked barley: its loose, inedible hull typically falls off during harvesting, which allows the processors to retain all of the bran and germ. Best of all, however, is black barley – an aubergine-coloured wholegrain that hails from Ethiopia and is grown in limited quantities in the USA. Fabulous stuff and very attractive in salads. I routinely beg people to grow and import it on your behalf.

CORN OR MAIZE

POSOLE • HOMINY • POPCORN • SWEETCORN

Corn is

sweet, milky, juicy, light, refreshing, tender, vegetal

It goes with

beef, cheese, squash, beans, tomatoes, chilli, coriander

It's good to eat for

fibre, magnesium, manganese, phosphorus, selenium, vitamins A and B1

Europeans of various nationalities have been sneering at corn or maize (*Zea mays*) for around 500 years, ever since Spain's Charles V decided it was a heathen's grain unfit for Christians. Bad call. Recent research is confirming what native Americans have known for years: that corn is a divine gift, or 'She Who Sustains Us', as one translation goes.

Turns out corn is particularly high in antioxidant phytonutrients and – here's a thing – different varieties and colours of corn (it grows in an astonishing range of decorator hues) offer different nutritional benefits. Corn is a good source of fibre and supports the growth of friendly bacteria in the large intestine. It improves blood sugar levels and has been found to be helpful for diabetics. It is also a good source of manganese, vitamin A and B vitamins, including folic acid.

The United States' love affair with corn began very early. In the spring after the *Mayflower* landed in 1620, friendly natives of the Wampanoag tribe taught the fledgling, starving Plymouth colony how to grow the crop, and its successful harvest was the basis of the first Thanksgiving. A key part of the natives' instruction was their system of farming, which saw corn, beans and squash – a perfectly balanced meal – grown together, then cooked together. Succotash, a classic dish of corn and

butter beans, still popular today, is said to have been served at the first Thanksgiving – as was popcorn.

Also important when it comes to maximizing the nutritional benefits of corn, particularly in Latin America, is alkali processing or nixtamalization – the preparation of corn with a calcium-hydroxide solution. The process, which involves soaking and cooking the corn with wood ash, seashells or crushed limestone, loosens the grain's outer hull, and makes its niacin and protein content more available to the body and the kernels easier to digest. Corn tortillas, hominy, posole and masa harina (dried posole meal or flour) are all products of this technique.

Most areas that have embraced corn enjoy it as mush in one form or another, whether that be the white polenta of Italy's Veneto, the mamlinga of Romania, mealiepap of South Africa or grits of the Southern USA. To understand the appeal, eschew quick-cook products in favour of the sweet fragrance and hearty texture of traditionally stoneground cornmeal. It takes longer to cook but the results, and health benefits, are far superior.

MILLET

Millet is
mild, beady, creamy, light, golden, sweet, alkaline

It goes with
beans, eggs, milk, cumin, parsley, green vegetables, berries

It's good to eat for
copper, fibre, iron, magnesium, manganese, phosphorus, potassium, protein, vitamins B1 and B3, zinc

Millet is the maiden aunt of the grain world. Oh sure, she had a bohemian past, hanging out with all those macrobiotic guys in the seventies, but it was brown rice they really wanted. These days it seems the best anyone can say about old millet is that she's alkaline.

This tendency to be seen as a poor second to rice is rather unfair. Millet scores better in nutritional analysis than rice or wheat, is gluten-free and the alkalinity means it is easy to digest – great for anyone feeling a bit under the weather. Compared to the main cereals, it is high in protein and iron, as well as being a good source of antioxidants and B vitamins, plus minerals including magnesium, potassium and zinc. Millet is reliable too. It grows so quickly that farmers can plant it late in the season, after other more popular crops have failed, and it will still mature in time for regular harvest. Kept dry and in the dark, millet grains can be stored for up to 20 years without attracting insect damage. It also hydrates well, so that a small amount of millet will feed more people than the same quantity of rice – in Nigeria, they call it 'hungry rice'.

I remember interviewing an esteemed Indian chef who confessed: 'Millet we use often. I don't want to tell you about it. It's poor man's food, not to the English palate.' Yet it has starred on the menu of Tokyo's Kozue restaurant for at least 15 years. There, the tiny beads are delicately bound with beaten egg, shaped into little dumplings filled with a few morsels of sweet aduki beans and lightly fried before being served floating on an intense red sauce. Many European country dishes and baked goods now made from cornmeal, rice or wheat were formerly cooked with millet – polenta is one of them – so surely it's time to let the old prejudices go.

Millet grains generally taste best toasted for a few minutes before boiling. If you want to sprout millet, you must buy grain marked 'unhulled'; it looks like it is wearing a shiny plastic coat. Millet flour can be delicious – a great addition to cakes and breads – but it turns rancid fairly quickly and most of what is on sale is past its best, leading to inevitable disappointment on cooking and eating. Therefore, only buy millet flour from a store with a very high turnover, and buy in small quantities. If you want to use millet flour regularly, consider grinding your own – it's easy to do using the grinding attachment of most modern food processors.

BUCKWHEAT

KASHA

Buckwheat is
rich, hearty, meaty, pungent, earthy, dark, angular

It goes with
poultry, fish, shellfish, onions, mushrooms, cream, maple syrup

It's good to eat for
calcium, copper, fibre, magnesium, manganese, phosphorus, protein, vitamins B2 and B3

Buckwheat is the anchovy of the grain world. You either love it or hate it. People who hate buckwheat can't understand how others can bear it, while those who love it tend to want it in everything and can't figure out what everyone else's problem is.

The first thing to know is that buckwheat (*Fagopyrum esculentum*) is not wheat and not even related to it. It is the seed of a leafy plant and, like many of the world's less popular grains, is easy to grow in poor soil and difficult climates, suiting the cold particularly. Depending on the variety and area, buckwheat takes only 60–120 days to grow, allowing some farmers to produce two crops in a season.

The earliest archaeological signs of its cultivation are from Japanese sites dated 3,500–5,000BC but it is still thought that the Chinese introduced it to Japan. In both cases, they were quick to grind it for use in noodle dough rather than serve it whole as the Russians and other Eastern Europeans do.

Contrast the refined, elegant, slippery soba noodle dishes of Japan with the rib-stickiness of, say, a Jewish casserole of beef brisket, marrow bones, potatoes, onion and buckwheat kernels. The unifying characteristic of these dishes is comfort quality. Even in Japan, buckwheat's role is to provide hearty tucker, and to gain maximum nourishment, the Japanese drink the soba's starchy cooking water mixed with the last of their noodles' dipping sauce.

Buckwheat is a good source of protein and a rare vegetarian opportunity to enjoy the fifth taste sensation of meaty savouriness, umami. In eating buckwheat you'll benefit from its high level of rutin – which increases blood circulation and helps prevent heart disease – plus lysine, B vitamins, calcium, phosphorus and other minerals. Buckwheat is also considered good for strengthening the kidneys and balancing blood sugar levels.

When past its best, buckwheat turns dark and its flavour becomes too strong, even for devoted fans. Make sure you buy only pale flour (the best is white, like talcum), and light olive-coloured buckwheat grains, ideally in see-through packets. Avoid bags labelled 'kasha' – these are pre-roasted, reddy-brown buckwheat of indeterminate age, and a non-convenience product. Toasting the kernels yourself takes only a couple of minutes and is very easy to do – simply heat some oil in a saucepan, add the buckwheat and cook, stirring, until it is browned and fragrant. A traditional Jewish method that keeps the grains distinct is to toss them in beaten egg first.

QUINOA

Quinoa is
pearlescent, beady, crunchy, bitter, astringent, grassy, mild

It goes with
shellfish, beef, spring onions, soy sauce, vinaigrette, grapes, citrus

It's good to eat for
amino acids, calcium, copper, fibre, folate, iron, magnesium, manganese, phosphorus, protein, vitamins B1, B6 and E

The popularity of quinoa among the affluent middle class is literally a joke. Witness the antics of Quinoa, Chevron, Sriracha and pals on Tiffany Beveridge's Pinterest board My Imaginary Well-Dressed Toddler Daughter and the spin-off book *How to Quinoa: Life Lessons from My Imaginary Well-Dressed Daughter*.

You don't need me to tell you that quinoa is a superfood – everybody's talking about it. *Chenopodium quinoa* is high in protein, with a great balance of amino acids, and boasts high levels of calcium, iron, fibre, B vitamins, vitamin E and phosphorus. Being a seed, rather than a cereal grain, it's also relatively high in fat and a good source of oil.

Apart from corn, no other grain comes in such a fine range of trendy decorator colours to tempt professional cooks and dinner party hosts. Ivory white or pale gold quinoa are the norm, but we increasingly see black and red too. The species also boasts green, pink, orange and purple varieties. Sprout the seeds, if you like, for use in salads, letting them turn green before eating. Distribution of quinoa flour has steadily improved as it has become recognized as a good non-wheat flour. It has a wonderful texture and produces particularly tender pancakes; however, you might find that the taste is one that needs to be acquired.

Quinoa tastes a lot better than it did 15 years ago. Improvements in processing mean it doesn't need to be rinsed so assiduously to remove the bitter-tasting residue of its natural protective coating saponin. The combination of soft, pearly bead and crunchy spiral tail is at first startling, but adds interest to salads, porridges, soups and puddings that most other grains can't match. Also attractive is the fact that, unlike other similarly virtuous wholegrains, quinoa can be cooked in just 10 minutes – faster than refined white rice, yet with a similarly light effect on the palate.

Quinoa is relatively easy to grow, thriving in mountainous regions, poor soil conditions and very dry climates. In addition to its native Peru and Bolivia, it is farmed in other parts of South America and in the USA, Canada, Australia and the UK. You may be able to grow it in your own backyard by paying it very little attention, and if you do, pick the plant's young green leaves to eat raw in salads or cook as for spinach. Expect to be hearing more about quinoa's little cousin kañiwa (*Chenopodium pallidicaule*) too. It offers all the health advantages of quinoa without the acrid saponin coating and is already being used in processed foods from Bolivia aimed at the European vegan market.

AMARANTH

Amaranth is
fine, light, gritty, spongy, sticky, herbaceous, malty

It goes with
corn, black beans, chilli, milk, honey, apple, coconut, chocolate

It's good to eat for
amino acids, calcium, copper, fibre, iron, magnesium, manganese, phosphorus, protein, selenium, vitamins B6 and E

Drive through the countryside of the western United States, especially California and Arizona, and you may notice a reddish weed growing unobtrusively by the side of the road. Look more closely, however, and you will find proof that weeds are merely displaced or misunderstood plants. This is amaranth, a revered leaf-cum-grain of the Aztecs, a pretty annual herb with red-crimson flowers. It may not be well known or widely consumed, but it is simply sitting there by the side of the road – and in an increasing number of organic food shops – waiting to be rediscovered.

The tiny, sand-like seeds – there are around 40,000–500,000 per plant – have the same flying saucer shape as quinoa, with an equatorial ring (said to be where the nutrients reside) that uncurls during cooking. Quinoa and amaranth have comparable health benefits too, but their behaviour in the kitchen is entirely different. Amaranth turns sticky (by which I mean downright gluey) when simmered in liquid. The grains can be cooked whole into a mild-tasting gruel or porridge that is highly digestible and therefore nourishing for the ill (I'm making it sound delicious, aren't I). Grinding them for use in flatbreads, cakes and drinks is common; so too is popping the grains, in which case they are made into sweets and snacks and included in breakfast cereals.

In general, I prefer to use amaranth as a true seed, quickly and easily stirred into doughs to give crunch. Because the seeds are so small, the sieve needed to rinse and drain them must be very fine – you may decide it's simply more practical to enjoy amaranth's health benefits in ready-made products.

But it's worth checking out. Amaranth has an impressive amino acid profile including lysine and methionine, making it a great vegetarian source of protein. It boasts twice the calcium content of milk, thrice the fibre of wheat and consumption is thought to actively lower cholesterol thanks to its tocotrienols, a type of vitamin E.

The leaves of the plant are an extremely good source of iron – better, in fact, than spinach or kale – and this is most likely how you will be seeing a lot more amaranth in future: stir-fried, steamed, tossed into salads or sprouted into microcress. Amaranth is a supergrain, yes, but also a super (reddish) green.

WILD RICE

....

Wild rice is

spiky, nutty, chewy, elegant, earthy, meaty, fragrant

....

It goes with

mushrooms, celery, poultry, fish, nuts, cream, orange, parsley

....

It's good to eat for

essential fatty acids, fibre, folate, magnesium, phosphorus, protein, vitamins B3 and B6, zinc

....

Wild rice, which is harvested from water grasses, can be found growing naturally in most states of the US and is the only grain native to North America. These days the majority of 'wild rice' on sale is farmed, although there are a few Native Americans, such as the Ojibwe of Saskatchewan and Minnesota, who continue to collect wild rice by hand from the wild. They go out in small canoes during late August and early September and smack or beat the water grasses to extract the grains. For some, harvesting is a spiritually important ritual, for others a means of acquiring a personal supply and having a nice day out with the family.

Archaeological evidence indicates that wild rice has been an important native food for at least 1,000 years, though the Ojibwe have been harvesting it only for the past 300 or so. The ancient belief system suggests that wild rice was a gift because it was not sown by people; it simply appeared in the water when the spirits wanted to bestow it.

In fact, wild rice was so difficult to grow and harvest that the first cultivated wild rice paddy was not established until the 1950s.

And that is why wild rice usually costs a lot more than other grains. If you find it sold inexpensively, the pack will be likely to contain a high proportion of broken grains. To make it accessible, many companies sell wild rice as a small percentage of a grain mixture. In these cases, the wild rice will have been mechanically scratched so that its naturally long cooking time (45–60 minutes) is reduced to something on a par with the other grains in the pack. Apparently, this doesn't result in a significant loss of nutrients.

Invest in wild rice, however, and you'll find it gives a lot of bang for your buck. It is extremely filling thanks to its high protein and fibre levels and can help dieters consume fewer calories over the course of a day. A 2009 study shows that its antioxidant activity is 30 times greater than that of white rice. It lowers blood triglycerides and increases levels of the good HDL cholesterol. It has more essential fatty acids and more lysine and methionine (key amino acids) than other staple cereals. The folate content is excellent too, plus it is a good source of B vitamins and immunity-boosting zinc. And that's just the edited highlights.

Wild rice is attractive and tasty when popped (though puffed is a better description for the resulting pillow shapes), and commercially ground flour is available, although it seems a shame to compromise these elegant chocolate-black spikes.

TRITICALE

Triticale is
plump, juicy, sweet, rich, chewy, fruity, robust

It goes with
salmon, bacon, mushrooms, bitter greens, spring onions, carrots, apricots

It's good to eat for
copper, fibre, folate, magnesium, manganese, phosphorus, vitamins B1 and B3, zinc

Science fiction says more about the time in which it is written than the time it is written about. In 1967, triticale was cutting edge, an exciting new grain formed by crossing rye and wheat. A *Star Trek* scriptwriter extrapolated that in future it would be the only Earth grain that could grow on a barren planet called Sherman's Planet. Ensuring the safe transport of the triticale was a vital mission given – naturally – to Captain James T Kirk and the crew of the Starship Enterprise.

That episode, 'The Trouble with Tribbles', is one of the most popular in the television series' history and, maybe come Stardate 4523.3, triticale will indeed be a vital food crop. But despite the constant television reruns – and a growing appreciation that science fiction often becomes science fact – few people in the 21st century have heard of triticale, let alone eaten it.

Triticale is not a product of genetic engineering or a clever laboratory technique, but simple cross-pollination that could have happened in nature – more intricate breeding goes into wheat these days than has ever gone into triticale. The grain is especially suited to organic farming, as it demands few pesticides. There is not a wealth of information on triticale's health benefits, and recently developed varieties differ dramatically from older types of triticale, but it is, as might be expected, nutritionally on a par with wheat and rye, offering slightly higher quantities of protein and essential amino acids, plus good levels of phosphorus and folate and excellent levels of thiamine and magnesium.

Once people try triticale, they seem to like it, especially in porridges, pancakes and waffles. Triticale is a naturally sweet grain that does not absorb much water. Cakes and scones made from triticale flour are tender but can dry out quickly. For those people who prefer rye breads made with a portion of wheat flour, triticale conveniently obliterates the need to buy two varieties. The rolled flakes are a pleasantly flavoured addition to oatmeal porridge; used alone, their texture might be considered too chewy. In general, triticale can be used anywhere you would use wheat or rye, giving wheat foods a more distinctive flavour and rye foods a milder one. Try some.

CHIA

Chia is

slippery, pearly, gelatinous, crunchy, gritty

It goes with

berries, citrus, mango, coconut milk, chocolate, yogurt, syrup

It's good to eat for

calcium, essential fatty acids, fibre, manganese, phosphorus

There's a moment in *Sleepless in Seattle* when Tom Hanks's character is with a friend in a bar discussing how the dating scene has changed since he was last single. His friend mentions tiramisu.

'Well, what is it?'

'You'll see!'

'You better tell me. Some woman is gonna want me to do it to her and I'm not going to know what it is.'

Chia is a bit like that. Five years ago you hadn't even heard of it and now suddenly you're expected to do it everyday.

Well, the good news is that you don't have to do much. Chia (*Salvia hispanica*) is a tiny seed that doesn't actually need cooking. Just combine 2 tbsp black or white seeds with 6 tbsp liquid (milk, fruit juice or ready-made smoothie) and leave it to stand for 30 minutes before stirring again. A gelatinous coating will develop around the seeds and seemingly set or thicken the liquid.

Some enthusiasts in the running fraternity simply down dry shots of chia followed by a glass of water. Other athletes, plus raw foodists, vegans and nutrition-obsessed parents, love it for its ease of use and myriad health claims.

Chia is a great source of omega 3, fibre and important minerals including calcium, making it especially advantageous for anyone living dairy free. It may help to stabilize blood sugar, enhance bone and tissue growth and repair, and improve blood pressure in diabetics. It's worth noting, however, that a few people don't get on with chia, finding it goes straight through them.

It works well in cerealish breakfast bowls, smoothies and pancakes, plus in bread, biscuits and crackers where it will stay crunchy. It can be sprouted too for salads and garnishing. If you are soaking black chia, don't let it stand in mixtures any longer than overnight, as the colour will leach into the other ingredients. To avoid lumps, stir the liquid into the seeds, rather than the seeds into the liquid – or simply combine them in a jar and shake.

Chia's gelling properties have attracted vegan bakers looking for egg substitutes – grind 1 tbsp white seed and whisk the resulting meal with 3 tbsp warm water. Leave to stand until the texture is reminiscent of an egg. Some use chia or chia bran as a vegan and gluten-free thickener for stews. I prefer genuinely delicious ways to serve chia such as Valrhona dark chocolate ganache with tamarillos and chia in black cardamom syrup, from Auckland's Orphan's Kitchen.

SORGHUM

Sorghum is
juicy, sweet, pearly, plump, chewy, sturdy, mild

It goes with
ginger, chilli, garlic, chicken, cucumber, carrots, buttermilk, honey

It's good to eat for
fibre, magnesium, manganese, phosphorus, selenium, vitamin B3

I'm not alone in loving sorghum, but it sometimes feels like it. This gluten-free wholegrain – largeish white beads with the juicy crunchiness of wheat berries – is extraordinarily difficult to find in the UK; the bright white flour is a little easier and occasionally you may see red sorghum flour from India. There are signs of change, however. Daniel Patterson of the Michelin-starred Coi restaurant in San Francisco has featured popped sorghum on his menus and in his groundbreaking cookbook, while Oregon-based supplier Bob's Red Mill has put admirable marketing effort into raising its profile.

There's an increasing body of evidence that sorghum deserves all the superfood status of its better-known rivals. It is a rich source of phytochemicals, helpful in managing cholesterol, diabetes and insulin resistance, promoting cardiovascular health and reducing the risk of cancer. There are even signs that it may help treat melanoma.

Those who have had the good fortune to travel to areas of sorghum cultivation tend to be rather perplexed that it is not more widely available as food for home use. In South Africa it is malted and ground into Maltabella, a wonderful chocolatey-tasting porridge that is a favourite healthy breakfast and the kind of comforting family food that makes expatriates turn misty-eyed while reminiscing about home.

Sorghum is a close relative of sugar cane and there are several varieties, though *Sorghum bicolor* is the one suited to human consumption. It is widely used throughout Africa, and in the first millennium BC was taken as a foodstuff to India, where it remains a vital crop. It is a hardy crop, perfect for areas of low rainfall. Sorghum was introduced to America in the mid-19th century. Today, it is grown primarily as livestock feed and for making molasses, although it can be used in a variety of porridges, breads and snacks, and also eaten as a fresh vegetable.

TEFF

Teff is
sandy, crunchy, malty, grassy, deep, rich, gluey

It goes with
peaches, banana, spinach, mushrooms, pumpkin, nuts, lime

It's good to eat for
calcium, copper, fibre, iron, manganese, magnesium, phosphorus, protein, vitamins B1, B6 and C, zinc

Teff (*Eragrostis*) is so incy-wincy – around 0.7 mm in diameter – that it isn't possible to remove its bran and germ layers. When you see ivory 'white' teff grains or flour on sale, they are wholegrain, just the same as brown teff, but simply a different coloured seed.

It is not the easiest grain to cook with – you will need an extremely fine sieve to rinse or drain it – and, like amaranth, its texture on boiling is gluey, making it unsuitable for salads or pilafs. Our clue to its lack of versatility comes from its native Ethiopia, where teff is used almost exclusively to make injera, the national flatbread-cum-plate, and alcohol.

Still, it provides over two-thirds of human nutrition in that country and is eaten at every meal. Injera has a distinctively sour taste, because the flour is fermented for three days before cooking, but teff itself does not taste sour. The flour (which is gluten free) gives a sweet honeyed flavour to baked goods, while the wholegrains can be used to add a crunchy texture like that of poppy seeds.

Rumours that teff grain is especially high in iron are unfounded – apparently that confusion arose because soil mixes with the grain when it is threshed on the ground. Teff is, however, a fabulous source of calcium, vitamin C and resistant starch, which assists weight control, blood sugar levels and colon health.

Top Ethiopians sportsmen Haile Gebrselassie and Kenenisa Bekele attribute some of their success to the nutritional benefits of teff, and scientists are keen to explore its properties more as Ethiopia has generally very low rates of anaemia, osteoporosis, diabetes and coeliac disease. With teff now being grown in countries including Australia, Canada, the USA and South Africa, we are sure to be hearing much more about it.

FURTHER FIELDS

Here is a range of interesting foods that, if not actually grains, can be used in ways similar to the grains and grain products featured in this book. A few are included as possible variations on recipes. Some are hippy wholefood favourites; others have a more intriguing culinary heritage grounded in traditional regional dishes from around the world. None has hit the mass market big-time, but all are worthy of some further attention, as they add welcome nutritional variety to cooking and are increasingly available via the internet, fine food retailers and the better organic health food stores.

Black bean flour

I was extremely dubious about this flour to start with, mainly because the processors' marketing seemed to emphasize its use as an instant food ingredient for things like black bean dip and soup. My first attempt to make soup from the flour was not encouraging, precisely because it did taste like flour and needed long cooking, plus a good slug of sherry to get rid of that mealy quality. But I very much like black bean flour for savoury baking. Used in griddle cakes (see page 30), it makes a great base for canapés with a Tex-Mex or Cal-Ital twist: avocado, lime, salsa, coriander, sour cream – that sort of thing.

Research has shown that black beans have the most antioxidant activity gram for gram of any bean. Apparently, the darker the skin of the bean, the higher the flavonoid (powerful antioxidant) content, so they are theoretically better for you than white beans. Like all antioxidant-rich foods, black beans help protect the body against cell-damaging free radicals and therefore a number of degenerative and chronic diseases.

Chestnut flour

As more and more speciality Italian ingredients are becoming available in other countries, chestnut flour (sometimes sold as *farina dolce* or 'sweet flour') is increasingly easy to buy. Castagnaccio is a wonderful cake from Italy's Lucchesia province made from chestnut flour, pine kernels, sultanas, rosemary and olive oil. The ancient Romans combined chestnut flour with wheat for breads and biscuits, versions of which are still made today.

On the nutritional front, it is something of an unsung hero: great for essential amino acids, folate and other B-group vitamins, vitamin E, iron, potassium, magnesium and dietary fibre. I often mix it with plain wheat flour in sweet shortcrust pastry recipes for traybakes, and hearty cakes like Devonshire honey, ginger or traditional fruit cakes. It has a fairly rich flavour that you might think restricts it to adult consumption.

Chickpea flour (also known as garbanzo flour)

Flour made from chickpeas is a favourite ingredient of India and Italy, where it is known as besan and ceci flour respectively. In India it is made into fritter batter, snacks such as pakora and sweets such as laddu, and used as a thickening agent for curries.

The Italians use it for socca or farinata, a simple street-food pancake, also known as Calda! Calda! (meaning Hot! Hot!). The batter is a cinch – just stir together equal quantities of chickpea flour and water and add a little olive oil and salt, and maybe some cumin, garlic or fresh herbs. Leave it to stand for a couple of hours if you can. Recreating the smoky flavours of a Mediterranean wood fire involves 'frying' the batter under the grill, so that it is lightly charred and blistered – there are some good step-by-step recipe photographs for this on the internet.

Chickpea flour has many health benefits, including good levels of protein, folate and other B vitamins, plus useful iron and magnesium. It is naturally higher in fat than flours made from cereal grains.

Coconut flour
The paleo diet craze has got many people talking about coconut flour, which is ground from dried coconut meat after it has been used to make coconut milk. It is extremely high in fibre, and can significantly reduce cholesterol levels and the risk of developing heart disease, diabetes and some types of cancer. They are just the headline benefits – its components also promote good skin health, thyroid function and blood sugar levels, and strengthen the nervous system.

The key thing to note is that because it is so very high in fibre (something you can feel when working with it), coconut flour cannot be readily substituted for other flours in baking, even when it comprises only a percentage of the mixture. A little goes a long way, and coconut flour demands additional moisture to combat its absorbency, plus extra eggs to give structure to a batter. On the plus side, its natural sweetness may allow you to reduce the quantity of added sugar in a recipe.

Fava bean flour
Fava bean flour is high in protein, fibre and iron but has a strong bean flavour that needs to be mollified with other flours (processors generally recommend chickpea flour for this) and/or pre-toasting.

A study has shown that replacing half the wheat flour in peanut butter muffins with fava bean flour resulted in most participants thinking the 50:50 muffins tasted better than the same recipe baked with only wheat flour. Interestingly, in Europe

fava bean flour is used as a flour improver in breadmaking because it aids the elongation of gluten.

Hemp
Hemp seeds are edible and not narcotic. They are used as food in Japan, Iran, Poland and Russia, and are increasingly manufactured into wholefood products such as snack bars and ice cream. I like Sally Butcher's recipe for mackerel fillets coated in crushed hemp seeds, sesame, parsley and breadcrumbs, from *Persia in Peckham*. The mackerel is daubed in mustard and lemon before being flour-egg-and-breadcrumbed, then shallow fried in olive oil.

Flour made from hemp has an intense grassy flavour that reminds me of seaweed and spirulina, so its uses are limited. I suggest you try it somewhere before investing in it yourself. The label on my pack recommends using hemp flour to replace up to 5 per cent of the plain flour in baked goods. That would require making 80 batches of hemp flour pancakes in order to use up a 500g/1 lb 2oz bag. Hmmm. What's the use-by date on the packet?

Far more practical in my view is to get the health benefits of hemp (a fabulous ratio of omega 3s to omega 6s, high protein and fibre, B vitamins, iron, zinc…) from the seeds and a few minimally processed products rather than from the flour.

Job's tears (also known as adley)
Job's tears are a true grain, *Coix lacryma-jobi*, and are reportedly helpful for so many ailments that it's difficult to believe they're not already being touted as a superfood all around the world. As it is, they are very difficult to find in shops.

The unhulled grains are tear-shaped, hence the name, though once the hull is removed and polished the grains look a bit like peanuts with a wide groove running down one side. On simmering, they swell to resemble damp popcorn. Some health practitioners recommend drinking the cooking water with a little lemon juice and sugar or honey, rather like lemon barley water.

Job's tears are used in traditional Chinese medicine to combat cancer and problems with the nervous, respiratory, circulatory, urinary and digestive systems. They are high in fibre, iron, calcium and selenium, among other nutrients, and are said to improve the skin.

Native to Southeast Asia, and most widely grown in the Philippines, Job's tears have spread to countries including India, Spain, Portugal and Brazil. You can expect to be hearing much more about them in years to come.

Linseed (also known as flaxseed)

Linseed is occasionally eaten as a grain in India, but it is fast gaining popularity elsewhere as an addition to bread – not, incidentally, a new idea in Europe. In rugged, seeded baked goods it works well, and is an extremely nutritious source of fibre and essential fatty acids as well as pharmacological levels of flavonoids (powerful antioxidants), making linseed an important addition to the diet for those who won't or can't eat soya.

Vegan bakers use linseed as a replacement for eggs (it is normally less expensive than chia) because the gel it produces when ground and soaked in water mimics (poorly) the structural and emulsifying qualities eggs give to batters and cakes.

The seeds can also simply be ground and stirred into cereals, but both oil and meal turn rancid quickly. If you want to use it ground, it is essential to grind it yourself and use it immediately. Some people take linseed oil as a nutritional supplement. When purchasing linseed oil, always buy the smallest bottle you can find.

Lupins

It may be some time before lupins, with their spikes of colourful flowers, are taken seriously as a source of food. However, they can indeed be used in myriad ways and make a good flour that people with wheat and gluten allergies would do well to seek out. An increasing number of manufacturers are including lupin flour in alternative breads and pasta products, and as the industry has identified several marketable advantages of lupin over soya, you can expect to see much more of it. It is worth noting, however, that people with peanut allergies may also be allergic to lupin (and perhaps unaware of it because it is such an uncommon ingredient).

Lupin flour is high in protein and fibre and low in fat, can help reduce cholesterol levels and blood pressure, and improve bowel health – but that's true of a lot of grains. More unusual is that there are two studies indicating that lupin is an appetite suppressant; it increases feelings of fullness and helps reduce overall energy intake.

In speciality European delicatessens you may find lupini, which are pickled or dried and salted lupin seeds that look rather like yellow broad beans. A favourite of the Romans, they are used in southern Italy, Peru and the Middle East, and can be eaten as a cocktail snack or mezze dish.

Mesquite

Prosopis juliflora or *P. veluntina* is native to central America but under-utilized there as food, despite its excellent nutritional properties. It's better known as a source of fragrant wood for barbecues, and a plant from which bees make aromatic honey. The young green plant pods can be cooked whole as a vegetable, while the naturally sweet seeds (péchita) are traditionally ground into a yellowy flour or meal for flatbreads and gruel-type drinks.

In *Coming Home to Eat*, Gary Paul Nabhan tells us that mesquite was a principal ingredient in the diet of American desert peoples for around 10,000 years, and that early Spanish explorers liked it, but that it fell from favour during the 19th century. The use of mesquite for barbecues is controversial, as it involves cutting down trees that would be better left standing as a source of food – rich in lysine, calcium, iron, zinc and more – for local communities.

Peasemeal

A traditional ingredient of Scotland, peasemeal is a delicious yellow-brown flour made by roasting and then grinding yellow field peas. It is used like oat and barley meals, most simply made into brose by placing a handful in a bowl and covering it with hot milk, water or stock, then stirring in a dab of butter and some salt. Flavourings such as dried fruit may be added. Peasemeal is also used in griddle-baked bannocks or scones. From the food industry's perspective, its sweet flavour means it is readily incorporated into baked goods.

Peasemeal is rich in lysine, folate, thiamine and zinc, and high in protein and fibre too. The traditional British dish pease pudding, famous from the nursery rhyme, is made with dried peas rather than ground meal but is no less healthy.

Sago

As my friend Claire Clifton says, you'd tend to hope that if the cannibals of New Guinea were going to eat you, they'd have you with a nice red wine sauce, but no: the final insult is that you'd be served with sago. Used in parts of the Americas, India, Africa and throughout Southeast Asia, sago is manufactured from the stem of the sago palm, as well as some other palms, including the date palm.

Sago is good used in milk puddings as well as those made from dried or fresh fruit. It can also be added to soups. An immediate hit in Britain when it was first imported in the 18th century, it has declined in popularity, but recently drinks of pearl sago and tea (bubble tea) have acquired a cult following in the English-speaking world.

The health advantages of sago are so limited that it tends to be mixed with other foods (such as rice) to boost a dish's nutrition. In India, it is associated with fasting and used for its 'cooling properties' to treat excess bile production.

Soya flour

This rich, creamy and somewhat milk-flavoured flour made from soya beans is a common sight in health food stores. Its chief purpose is adding protein, flavonoids and moistness (for it is high in fat) to baked goods requiring a gluten-free replacement for wheat flour, or as a substitute for eggs.

However, it also makes things leaden and if possible soya flour should not comprise more than one-third of a baked item's dry ingredients. Coeliacs aside, I don't know any real cooks of any nationality who use soya flour. There are many wonderful ingredients and dishes of true culinary heritage that can be made from soya beans; this, like textured vegetable protein (TVP), isn't one of them.

Tapioca

When the English say tapioca they generally mean the milk pudding made from it, but it has other uses and the Brazilians, for example, make it into a delicious-sounding pudding with red wine or grape juice. Although it is granular, tapioca is in fact a highly processed product manufactured from a pulp that is made from the cassava root. The cassava is native to the Americas but has become an important ingredient in Asian and African cooking. Tapioca is available as small and large beads, flakes and flour, and is pretty much interchangeable with sago. Tapioca doesn't have the protein advantages of true grains, seeds and pulses, but it is high in fibre and can be a welcome source of iron.

Urad dal

These are skinned and split black lentils, though as the skin has been removed they do not look black but creamy-grey. Freshly ground urad dal are used in the cooking of southern India, most typically for idlis and dosa batter. They are also used almost like a spice, added to the oil at the beginning of making a dish along with mustard seeds, dried chillies and curry leaves.

In northern India the black lentils are often used whole. The use of the word dal indicates that the pulse has been split. In India, urad dal are attributed with all manner of health-boosting properties, from curing impotency to making hair thick and shiny. They are a good source of iron, magnesium, folate, protein and fibre.

COOKING GUIDE

Grain – per 225ml/1 cup	Stovetop liquid	Stovetop boiling time	Pressure-cooking liquid
Amaranth	3 cups	20 mins	2 cups
Barley, semi-pearled or pot	3 cups	45–75 mins	2¼ cups
Barley, white-pearled	2½–3 cups	20–30 mins	2¼ cups
Barley, grits or cracked	3 cups	20 mins	2¼ cups
Buckwheat, groats	2 cups	12–20 mins	n/a
Corn, coarse meal or polenta	3–4 cups	35–40 mins	2½ cups
Corn, grits	3–4 cups	30 mins	2½ cups
Corn, hominy or samp	3–4 cups	1½ hours	2½ cups
Corn, posole large	4 cups	2–3 hours	3 cups
Millet, hulled	3 cups	15–20 mins	2½ cups
Oats, wholegrain	4 cups	1–1¼ hours	2½ cups
Oatmeal, coarse or steel-cut	4 cups	45 mins	3½–4 cups
Oatmeal, medium	5 cups	30 mins	n/a
Quinoa	2 cups	12–15 mins	1¾ cups
Rice, pearled	2 cups	15–20 mins	1¾ cups
Rice, semi-pearled	2½ cups	25–30 mins	2 cups
Rice, wholegrain	3 cups	35–45 mins	1½ cups
Rye, wholegrain	4 cups	1–1¼ hours	2½ cups
Sorghum	3 cups	50–60 mins	3 cups
Teff	3 cups	20 mins	4 cups
Triticale, wholegrain	4 cups	1½–2 hours	3 cups
Wheat, bulgur	2 cups	20–30 mins	1½ cups
Wheat, cracked	3 cups	45–50 mins	2½ cups
Wheat, freekeh wholegrain	2½–3 cups	25–30 mins	2 cups
Wheat, freekeh cracked	2½–3 cups	10–15 mins	2 cups
Wheat, wholegrain	4 cups	2 hours	2½ cups
Wheat, semi-pearled	2½–3 cups	25–30 mins	2 cups
Wheat, pearled	2 cups	20 mins	1½ cups
Wild rice	4 cups	45–50 mins	3½ cups

Pressure-cooking time	Sensory cues	Yield
15–20 mins	Grains meld into a thick and gluey porridge	3 cups
45 mins	Grains expand to give a texture like crunchy, juicy berries	4¼ cups
15–20 mins	Grains swell to give a texture like juicy pillows	2¼ cups
15 mins	Grains are swollen, juicy and crunchy with an uneven, gritty texture	2¼ cups
n/a	Grains swell and soften, but retain texture of angular pebbles	n/a
20 mins	Tiny starch grains burst to give a blowsy, textured, thick mixture	2½ cups
20 mins	Grits become a thick, creamy paste	2½ cups
40–50 mins	Grains soften gradually to textured paste	2½ cups
50 mins	Grains burst open like a flower and are softly chewy	3 cups
8–10 mins	Grains puff up and soften to give a fine, light sandy texture	2½ cups
50 mins	Grains maintain their shape, but become tender and creamy	2½ cups
30 mins	Grains gradually meld into a thick paste with a hint of crunch	3½–4 cups
n/a	Grains gradually meld into a thick, slightly textured paste	n/a
5–7 mins	Equatorial bands uncurl and grains are pearlescent	3 cups
5–8 mins	Grains swell and become tender	2¼ cups
15 mins	Grains swell and reveal starchy interior with slight crunchiness	2¼ cups
30 mins	Grains swell and become tender, but offer resistance to bite	2¼ cups
40 mins	Grains swell to give a texture like crunchy, juicy berries	2½ cups
20–25 mins	Grains swell to give a texture like crunchy, juicy berries	2½ cups
3 mins	Grains meld into thick gluey porridge	3¾ cups
50–60 mins	Grains swell to give a texture like crunchy, juicy berries	2½ cups
10–12 mins	Grains swell and soften, but retain an even, pebble-like texture	3–3½ cups
40–45 mins	Grains are swollen, juicy and crunchy with an even, gritty texture	3½ cups
15–20 mins	Grains swell and become tender, but offer resistance to bite	3–3½ cups
7–8 mins	Grains are swollen and juicy with a gritty texture	3–3½ cups
40–50 mins	Grains swell to give a texture like crunchy, juicy berries	2⅔ cups
12–15 mins	Grains are swollen and softened, but still toothsome	2⅔ cups
8 mins	Grains swell to give a texture of firm, cooked pasta	2½ cups
20–25 mins	Grains split lengthways revealing fleshy white interior	2½ cups

NUTRITIONAL FACTS

Grain – per 100g (3½oz), uncooked	Calories	Carbohydrate (g)
Amaranth	391	63.1
Barley, wholegrain	301	64
Barley, semi-pearled or pot	346	76.4
Barley, white-pearled	360	83.6
Barley, meal	345	74.5
Buckwheat, groats	343	71.5
Buckwheat flour, wholemeal	335	70.6
Chia	486	42
Cornmeal, wholemeal yellow	362	76.9
Corn grits	371	79.6
Cornmeal, masa, enriched yellow	365	76.3
Cornmeal, fine white degermed	366	77.7
Millet	378	72.8
Millet flour	354	75.4
Oats, wholegrain	389	66.3
Oatmeal, medium	401	72.8
Quinoa	374	68.9
Rice, polished	361	86.8
Rice, wholegrain	357	81.3
Rye, wholegrain	335	69.8
Rye flour, dark	324	68.7
Rye flour, light	367	80.2
Sorghum	339	75
Teff	367	73
Triticale, wholegrain	336	72.1
Triticale flour, wholemeal	338	73.1
Wheat, bulgur	342	75.9
Wheat, freekeh wholegrain	345	72
Wheat, common wholegrain	335	72.7
Wheat, petit épeautre wholegrain	375	74.9
Wheat, Kamut wholegrain	359	68.2
Wheat, pearled such as Pasta Wheat	337	70.4
Wheat flour, refined	341	77.7
Wheat flour, wholemeal	310	63.9
Wild rice	365	74.3

Sources various; N = component is present in significant quantities, but figures are unreliable.

Fibre (g)	Protein (g)	Fat (g)	Gluten
2.9	15.3	7.1	No
17.3	10.6	2.1	Yes
10.4	10.7	2.2	Yes
5.9	7.9	1.7	Yes
10.1	10.5	1.6	Yes
10	13.2	3.4	No
10	12.6	3.1	No
34	17	31	No
7.3	8.1	3.6	No
1.6	8.8	1.2	No
9.6	9.3	3.8	No
7.4	8.5	1.6	No
8.5	11	4.22	No
N	5.8	1.7	No
10.6	16.9	6.9	Yes
6.3	12.4	8.7	Yes
5.9	13.1	5.8	No
2.2	6.5	1	No
3.8	6.7	2.8	No
14.6	14.8	2.5	Yes
22.6	14	2.6	Yes
14.6	8.4	1.4	Yes
6.3	11	3.3	No
8	13	2.4	No
N	13	2.1	Yes
14.6	13.2	1.8	Yes
18.3	12.3	1.3	Yes
16.5	12.6	2.7	Yes
2.1	12.3	1.9	Yes
7.7	11.8	2.9	Yes
1.8	17.3	2.6	Yes
6.7	11.3	1.1	Yes
3.6	9.4	1.3	Yes
8.6	12.7	2.2	Yes
7	13.2	1.7	No

SPROUTING

Grain	Soak	Rinse	Days	Length of sprout
Amaranth	3–5 hours	2 times per day	2–3 days	5mm–1cm/¼–½in
Barley	6–10 hours	3 times per day	2–3 days	5mm/¼in
Buckwheat	15 minutes	every hour for 4 hours, then 3 times per day	2–3 days	1–2.5cm/½–1in
Chia	12 hours	spritz to keep moist	7 days	2.5cm/1in
Millet	5–7 hours	3 times per day	2 days	3mm/⅛in
Oat	3–5 hours	2 times per day	2 days	5mm/¼in
Quinoa	2–4 hours	3 times per day	2–4 days	5mm–3cm/¼–1¼in
Rice	6–10 hours	3 times per day	2–3 days	3mm/⅛in
Rye	6–10 hours	2 times per day	2–3 days	5mm–1cm/¼–½in
Teff	3–4 hours	2 times per day	1–2 days	3–4mm/⅛in
Triticale	6–10 hours	2 times per day	2–3 days	5mm–1cm/¼–½in
Wheat	6–10 hours	2 times per day	2–3 days	5mm–1cm/¼–½in

See page 65 for sprouting instructions.
Chart is for indoor jar or tray sprouting, not for
the production of wheatgrass. In all cases it
is essential to purchase wholegrains
specifically for sprouting from a specialist
supplier. Adequate drainage is essential
to prevent mould growth. Grains are
unlikely to sprout successfully in
hot weather.

Adapted from chart by *Sprouting
Publications*, plus various sources.

INDEX

adley 181-2
African corn and peanut patties 123
alegria 151
allspice
   chicken with freekeh 92
   freekeh pilaf 105
almonds
   almond cake 140
   teff lemon cream bars 138
   torta sbrisolona 146
amaranth 174, 184, 186
   alegria 151
   Americas bread 45
   bellies 150
Americas bread 45
Anzac biscuits 152
apples
   baked caramel apples with spelt 135
   Bircher muesli 24
apricots
   farro with apricots, pomegranate and
      pine kernels 23
asparagus
   brown rice and chia lunch bowl 59
   rye gnocchi with spring vegetables 74
Ayurvedic medicine 9

bacon
   herring in oatmeal 109
   rye gnocchi with spring vegetables 74
banana and coconut pudding 129
bannocks, Orkney-style 40
barley 169, 184, 186
   barley grit couscous 68
   barley 'risotto' 90
   barley and yogurt salad 64
   braised barley with lemon and spices
      117
   Finnish oven porridge 26
   John's granola 14
   lovely lamb stew 95
   mushroom ragout with barley 96
   ogokbap 119
   Persian-style barley soup 55
barley flour
   barley bread 44
   Norwegian flatbr¢d 47
   Orkney-style bannocks 40
beans
   brown rice and chia lunch bowl 59
   ogokbap 119
   rye gnocchi with spring vegetables 74
   sponzo salad 60

summer minestrone 49
beef
   grilled beefsteak 160
   poached beef 161–2
bellies 150
beremeal flour
   oatcakes 156
   Orkney-style bannocks 40
berries
   quick berry compote 163
Bircher muesli 24
black bean flour 180
Breton crêpes 27
broccoli
   rye gnocchi with spring vegetables 74
   uppma 114
buckwheat 172, 184, 185
   buckwheat noodles 72
   crab with buckwheat and spelt 89
   Japanese soba porridge 81
   kasha 111
buckwheat flour
   buckwheat, cacao and apricot
      ice-cream sandwiches 132
   griddle cakes 30
buckwheat sprouts 65
   hazelnut and feta sprout salad 63
burgers, grain 78
butter, shellfish 89, 160

cacao
   buckwheat, cacao and apricot
      ice-cream sandwiches 132
carrots
   genmai gomoku 91
   lovely lamb stew 95
   roast carrots with dill granola 120
cavolo nero
   farro with chestnuts and cavolo nero
      124
chard
   sponzo salad 60
cheese
   best-ever cheesecake filling 163
   cream cheese frosting 163
   hard polenta 82
   hazelnut and feta sprout salad 63
   layered cornmeal with spicy tomato
      sauce 85
   rice and ricotta salad 62
   rye and cheese crackers 155
   soft, creamy polenta 83
   sponzo salad 60

sweetcorn fritters 80
sweetcorn risotto 86
chestnuts
   chestnut flour 180
   farro with chestnuts and cavolo nero
      124
chia 177
   brown rice and chia lunch bowl 59
   quinoa and chia pancakes with
      mango and basil compote 29
chicken
   chicken with freekeh 92
   chicken jus 162
   farro, pine kernel and sultana sauté
      106
   grain-based stuffings for 103
   grilled chicken 160
   mixed crumb coatings for 110
   posole verde 102
   quinoa, chicken and spinach soup 52
   roasted chicken 161
   sorghum chicken salad with coconut
      and lime 56
chickpea flour 180–1
chillies 162
chocolate
   chocolate polenta soufflé 137
   chocolate spelt cake 143
choosing grains 8
Claire's Mediterranean cornbread 42
coconut
   alegria 151
   Anzac biscuits 152
   banana and coconut pudding 129
   barley 'risotto' 90
   coconut broth 163
   crunchy oat and coconut slice 149
   oatmeal and pecan cake 144
   sorghum chicken salad with coconut
      and lime 56
   sticky black rice with coconut and
      tofu 20
   sticky black rice custard 128
coconut flour 181
cooking guide 184–5
cooking times 10
corn 170, 184, 186
   corn ice cream 125
   corn stock 51
   sweetcorn fritters 80
   sweetcorn risotto 86
corn ice cream 125
corn stock 51

corn tortillas 37
cornmeal
    African corn and peanut patties 123
    chocolate polenta soufflé 137
    Claire's Mediterranean cornbread 42
    cornmeal porridge 16
    hard polenta 82
    layered cornmeal with spicy tomato
      sauce 85
    New Orleans pain de riz 39
    soft, creamy polenta 83
    torta sbrisolona 146
    wild rice waffles 33
crab with buckwheat and spelt 89
crumb crust 163

dashi 162–3
dill
    roast carrots with dill granola 120
Dutch honey cake 36

farro 165
    farro with apricots, pomegranate and
      pine kernels 23
    farro with chestnuts and cavolo nero
      124
    farro, pine kernel and sultana sauté
      106
    multigrain scones 41
    summer minestrone 49
fava bean flour 181
fennel
    spaghetti with sardines and fennel
      69
fibre in food 8
Finnish oven porridge 26
fish
    barley grit couscous 68
    brown rice and chia lunch bowl 59
    buckwheat stuffing for 111
    grilled fish 160–1
    mixed crumb coatings for 110
    pan-roasted fish 161
flaxseed 182
food intolerances 8
freekeh 165, 184, 186
    chicken with freekeh 92
    freekeh pilaf 105
    grain burgers 78
    stuffing for chicken 103
freezing grains 10
fritters, sweetcorn 80

gammon
    grünkohl 100
genmai gomoku 91
Graham crackers 154
grain burgers 78
granola, John's 14
grapes
    milhassou 126

quinoa, cashew and grape salad 67
griddle cakes 30
grünkohl 100

health and grains 8–10
hemp 181
herring in oatmeal 109
hominy
    African corn and peanut patties 123

ice cream
    buckwheat, cacao and apricot
      ice-cream sandwiches 132
    corn ice cream 125
    oatmeal praline ice cream 131

Japanese soba porridge 81
Job's tears 181–2
John's granola 14

kasha 111
Korean chilli sauce 162

lamb
    lovely lamb stew 95
    roast lamb 161
    skirlie stuffing for 113
lemons
    braised barley with lemon and spices 117
    teff lemon cream bars 138
lentils
    uppma 114
limes
    sorghum chicken salad with coconut
      and lime 56
    spicy prawn and quinoa cakes 77
linseed 182
lupins 182

maize see corn
mangoes
    quinoa and chia pancakes with
      mango and basil compote 29
masa harina
    bellies 150
    corn tortillas 37
mealie candy 159
mesquite 182
milhassou 126
millet 171, 184, 186
    grain burgers 78
    millet congee 50
    ogokbap 119
    savoury millet cake 112
    sponzo salad 60
    uppma 114
millet flour
    milhassou 126
miso
    brown rice and miso porridge with
      pears and walnuts 19

muesli, Bircher 24
muffins, old-fashioned 34
multigrain scones 41
mung bean sprouts
    hazelnut and feta sprout salad 63
mushrooms
    farro with chestnuts and cavolo nero
      124
    genmai gomoku 91
    mushroom ragout with barley 96
    wild mushroom sauce 162
mussels
    shellfish and saffron stew 99

New Orleans pain de riz 39
noodles, buckwheat 72
Norwegian flatbr¢d 47
nutritional facts 186–7
nuts
    African corn and peanut patties 123
    Bircher muesli 24
    hazelnut and feta sprout salad 63
    oatmeal and pecan cake 144
    quinoa, cashew and grape salad 67
    stuffing for chicken 103
    see also almonds; pine kernels;
      walnuts

oatmeal 184, 186
    grain burgers 78
    grünkohl 100
    herring in oatmeal 109
    mealie candy 159
    Norwegian flatbr¢d 47
    oatcakes 156
    oatmeal and pecan cake 144
    oatmeal porridge 17
    oatmeal praline ice cream 131
    skirlie 113
oats 168, 184, 186
    Anzac biscuits 152
    Bircher muesli 24
    crunchy oat and coconut slice 149
    John's granola 14
    mixed crumb coatings 110
    pumpkin and sage pudding 116
    roast carrots with dill granola 120
ogokbap 119
olives
    Claire's Mediterranean cornbread 42
    spaghetti with tomatoes, olives and
      walnuts 70
Orkney-style bannocks 40

pastry
    rich sweet pastry 163
    wholemeal pastry case 136
pears
    brown rice and miso porridge with
      pears and walnuts 19
peasemeal 182–3

peppers
  Claire's Mediterranean cornbread 42
  roast bell peppers 162
  uppma 114
Persian-style barley soup 55
pine kernels
  Claire's Mediterranean cornbread 42
  farro with apricots, pomegranate and
    pine kernels 23
  farro, pine kernel and sultana sauté 106
  roast carrots with dill granola 120
polenta
  chocolate polenta soufflé 137
  hard polenta 82
  soft, creamy polenta 83
pomegranate
  farro with apricots, pomegranate and
    pine kernels 23
popcorn 157
pork
  posole verde 102
porridge 168
  cornmeal porridge 16
  oatmeal porridge 17
posole verde 102
potatoes
  Americas bread 45
  lovely lamb stew 95
  rye gnocchi with spring vegetables 74
prawns
  grilled prawns 160–1
  shellfish and saffron stew 99
  spicy prawn and quinoa cakes 77
protein in grains 8
pumpkin and sage pudding 116

quinoa 173, 184, 186
  Americas bread 45
  quinoa, cashew and grape salad 67
  quinoa and chia pancakes with
    mango and basil compote 29
  quinoa, chicken and spinach soup 52
  spicy prawn and quinoa cakes 77
  stuffing for chicken 103

raisins
  baked caramel apples with spelt 135
  Bircher muesli 24
  freekeh pilaf 105
  John's granola 14
rice 166, 184, 186
  brown rice and chia lunch bowl 59
  brown rice and miso porridge with
    pears and walnuts 19
  genmai gomoku 91
  grain burgers 78
  New Orleans pain de riz 39
  ogokbap 119
  rice and ricotta salad 62
  sticky black rice with coconut and
    tofu 20

sticky black rice custard 128
  sweetcorn risotto 86
rye 167, 184, 186
rye flour
  Dutch honey cake 36
  gnocchi with spring vegetables 74
  Graham crackers 154
  Norwegian flatbrɛd 47
  old-fashioned muffins 34
  rye and cheese crackers 155

sage
  pumpkin and sage pudding 116
sago 183
salmon
  brown rice and chia lunch bowl 59
samp
  African corn and peanut patties 123
sardines
  spaghetti with sardines and fennel 69
sausages
  grünkohl 100
scallops
  shellfish and saffron stew 99
scones, multigrain 41
shellfish butter 89, 160
shellfish and saffron stew 99
shellfish stock 160
skirlie 113
soaking grains 10
sorghum 178
  sorghum chicken salad with coconut
    and lime 56
Soweto grey bread 46
soya flour 183
spaghetti
  spaghetti with sardines and fennel 69
  spaghetti with tomatoes, olives and
    walnuts 70
spelt 165
  baked caramel apples with spelt 135
  chocolate spelt cake 143
  crab with buckwheat and spelt 89
  summer minestrone 49
spinach
  African corn and peanut patties 123
  crab with buckwheat and spelt 89
  quinoa, chicken and spinach soup 52
  rye gnocchi with spring vegetables 74
sponzo salad 60
spring greens
  grünkohl 100
sprouts/sprouting 65, 188
storing grains 10
sultanas
  Bircher muesli 24
  farro, pine kernel and sultana sauté
    106
  freekeh pilaf 105
  John's granola 14
summer minestrone 49

tapioca 183
teff 179
  teff lemon cream bars 138
toffee sauce 163
tofu
  genmai gomoku 91
  sticky black rice with coconut and
    tofu 20
tomatoes
  indispensable tomato sauce 162
  layered cornmeal with spicy tomato
    sauce 85
  spaghetti with tomatoes, olives and
    walnuts 70
  sponzo salad 60
  torta sbrisolona 146
tortillas, corn 37
triticale 176, 184, 186

uppma 114
urad dal 183

vanilla
  banana and coconut pudding 129
  sticky black rice custard 128
  torta sbrisolona 146

waffles, wild rice 33
wakame
  brown rice and chia lunch bowl 59
walnuts
  baked caramel apples with spelt 135
  brown rice and miso porridge with
    pears and walnuts 19
  chocolate spelt cake 143
  mealie candy 159
  spaghetti with tomatoes, olives and
    walnuts 70
wheat 165, 184, 186
wheat flakes
  mixed crumb coatings 110
wheatberries
  farro with apricots, pomegranate and
    pine kernels 23
  multigrain scones 41
  wheatberry and honey cake 145
wholemeal pastry case 136
wild rice 175, 184, 186
  Americas bread 45
  multigrain scones 41
  shellfish and saffron stew 99
  stuffing for chicken 103
  wild rice waffles 33

yogurt
  barley and yogurt salad 64
  Bircher muesli 24

ACKNOWLEDGEMENTS

I'd like to thank once again everyone who helped me produce *A Cook's Guide to Grains* all those years ago and all those who have been so supportive of the publication since then. I am blessed not only that Stephanie Jackson saw fit to approach me about it, but that she and Jonathan Christie (who had already treated me to Angie Lewin's wonderful illustrations on the second edition) assigned such a crack team to the project. Ellie Smith was a font of sound judgement and calm throughout her time on this, and working with Liz and Max Haarala Hamilton, Kat Mead, Janet Stone and Jaz Bahra at Warehouse Studios was a joy; I have never felt in such safe hands. Thanks also to Jane Ellis, who kept things ticking over, and Polly Poulter, who saw it through to publication. Nick Saltmarsh, Peter Gordon and Helena Puolakka graciously spared some time to help clarify my thoughts on this new book. I must again pay tribute to Glynn Christian who first got me thinking seriously about grains with his *New Delicatessen Food Handbook*, a work that continues to surprise me with its breadth and depth of coverage. Special thanks to Mike Lucy for his generous support, and to the team at Company of Cooks. My husband David gave excellent feedback during recipe testing; I'm very fortunate that he is so easy-going about these things. So, too, my parents. Finally, Claire Clifton is, as she has been for nearly 20 years, one of my most valued sounding boards and dearest friends and it is to her that this book is dedicated.

About the author

From the rice paddies of Northern Thailand and Calasparra, to the stone mills of Brittany, Gloucestershire and Cork, Shinjuku soba houses, and the markets of Yucatán – Jenni Muir has travelled the world applying her restaurant critic's palate to our most important and nutritious staple foods. The former editor of *Time Out London Eating & Drinking Guide* and one-time chairperson of The Guild of Food Writers, Jenni's work has appeared in a wide range of publications including *BBC Good Food*, *Country Living*, the *Sunday Times*, and the *Independent*. Her critically acclaimed book *A Cook's Guide to Grains* was nominated for the Glenfiddich, André Simon and Guild of Food Writers awards; this was followed with various luxury food and travel guides including *The Guest List*, which featured on Richard & Judy's Book Club. Jenni lives in London and Bath with her husband and daughter, while also trying to visit her native Australia as much as possible.

You can follow Jenni on Twitter @jennimuir
For more on wholegrains and other good foods visit www.nourish.co.uk

Publisher: Stephanie Jackson
Senior Editor: Ellie Smith
Editor: Pollyanna Poulter
Art Director: Jonathan Christie
Designer: Jaz Bahra
Photography: Liz & Max Haarala Hamilton
Illustrations: Angie Lewin
Home Economy & Food Styling: Kat Mead
Production Controller: Sarah-Jayne Johnson

An Hachette UK Company
www.hachette.co.uk

First published in Great Britain in 2014 by Hamlyn, a division of Octopus Publishing Group Ltd, Endeavour House, 189 Shaftesbury Avenue London, WC2H 8JY
www.octopusbooks.co.uk

This is a revised and updated edition of *A Cook's Guide to Grains*.

Copyright © Octopus Publishing Group Ltd 2014

ISBN: 978-0-600-62992-4

A CIP catalogue record for this book is available from the British Library

Printed and bound in China

1 2 3 4 5 6 7 8 9 10

Standard level spoon measurements are used in all recipes. 1 tablespoon = 15ml spoon. 1 teaspoon = 5ml spoon

Ovens should be preheated to the specified temperature – if using a fan-assisted oven, follow the manufacturer's instructions for adjusting the time and temperature.

Fresh herbs should be used unless otherwise stated. Large eggs should be used unless otherwise stated. Freshly ground black pepper should be used unless otherwise stated.

This book includes dishes made with nuts and nut derivatives. It is advisable for people with known allergic reactions to nuts and nut derivatives or those who may be potentially vulnerable to these allergies, such as pregnant and nursing mothers, invalids, the elderly, babies and children, to avoid dishes made with these. It is prudent to check the labels of all pre-prepared ingredients for the possible inclusion of nut derivatives.